SURVIVING

On The TEXAS Frontier

SURVIVING

On The TEXAS Frontier

The Journal of an Orphan Girl
in San Saba County

Sarah Harkey Hall

Introduction by
Paula Mitchell Marks

EAKIN PRESS ★ Austin, Texas

Published in the United States of America
By Eakin Press
An Imprint of Sunbelt Media, Inc.
P.O. Drawer 90159 ★ Austin, TX 78709-0159

ISBN 0-89015-986-6

2   3   4   5   6   7   8   9

Library of Congress Cataloging-in-Publication Data

Hall, Sarah Harkey, 1857–1908
    Surviving on the Texas frontier : the journal of a frontier orphan girl in San Saba County, 1857–1908 / by Sarah Harkey Hall : introduction by Paula Mitchell Marks. — 1st ed.
        p.   cm.
    Includes bibliographical references and index.
    ISBN 0-89015-986-6 : $17.95
    1. Hall, Sarah Harkey, 1857–1908 — Diaries. 2. Women pioneers — Texas — San Saba County — Diaries. 3. Orphans — Texas — San Saba County — Diaries. 4. Pioneers — Texas — San Saba County — Diaries. 5. San Saba County (Tex.) — Social life and customs. 6. Frontier and pioneer life — Texas — San Saba County. I. Title.
F392.S24H285   1996
976.4'68061'092–dc20
[B]   94-12612
                                                                        CIP

Contents

Sarah Harkey Hall

Foreword

[The foreword is a compilation of submissions by three
of Sarah Harkey Hall's descendants.]

This is the life story of my great-grandmother, Sarah
Caroline Harkey. She married David C. Hall. Her father was
Daniel Riley Harkey. Her mother was Margaret E. Smith. Daniel
Harkey was born in 1829. His great-great-grandfather was
Johanas Herche of Dutch ancestry who traveled from Holland to
England, where he changed his name to Harkey. He crossed the
Atlantic on the ship *Lidie* and arrived in Philadelphia in 1713. He
settled in North Carolina and lived until 1769, when he received
a King's Grant from King George III for a Colonial Plat (or plan-
tation) in Craven County, South Carolina. Some of the Harkeys
moved to San Saba County in 1855 one year before its organiza-
tion.

Sarah, whom everyone called Diden because she was the first
of all the brothers and sisters to say "I diden" when asked by their
parents which one had done some mischievous deed, was the
fifth of thirteen children left orphans when their parents died
within a month of each other.

The boys were Joe, Jim, John, Levi, Jeff, Dee, Mose, and Eli.
The girls were Jane, Julia, Sarah, Martha, and Annie.

They had a very hard life after their parents died. The older
kids took care of the younger. They were hungry a lot, scared of
Indian attacks and, since there were few families settled around
Richland Springs, no one could help them much. I have included
a picture of the old oak tree that Diden hid in when she was a
little girl when an Indian rode up under it looking for horses and
children to steal. The tree is on Byron Lewis' farm one mile east
of Richland Springs where the Harkey children lived.

Sarah and Dave Hall's children were Amy Elizabeth Hall, who was my grandmother, Matthew, Burney, Dee, Minor, and Essie.

My grandmother, Amy, married Louis Thomas Warren and they had one child, my mother, Beulah Mable Warren. She married my dad, Lee Doran Lambert, and I am their only child. My dad died in 1973 and my mother lives in Odessa, Texas, is ninety-six years old and lives alone.

I live in Kingsland, Texas, on Lake LBJ with my husband, Royce Henry. I had three girls by my first husband, Johnnie Ray Brown from Richland Springs. They are Jan Brazell, Tana Gray, and Joylyn Tillotson, who is deceased. Royce and I have one daughter, Lisa LeAnn Holloway, who lives in Tracy, California. (Thanks to my daughter Jan and her husband Delton, for typing the manuscript and preparing the disk.)

I thought the readers might enjoy a recipe we found written by Dave Hall, Sarah's husband. It's for trap bait.

> 4 oz. of wolf urine
> anal glands of wolf
> gall of wolf
> 4 oz. glycerin
> Mix and bottle.

MARIDELL LAMBERT HENRY

I am the granddaughter of Sarah Harkey Hall. My earliest memory was when I was four years old.

My father thought he would like to move to Hope, New Mexico, where my grandparents had moved to. We traveled by covered wagon, which took weeks. I remember gathering "cow chips" to build fires to cook our meals. My mother took typhoid fever and almost died. All her hair fell out. When she was able to travel we headed for home, Richland Springs.

When I was nine years old my grandmother, Diden, became very ill and my mother and I went by train to Hope. We took the train from Rochelle, Texas. It was Christmas time and when we arrived in Carlsbad, New Mexico, we went to a hotel where they had Christmas dinner with all the trimmings. I remember how long that table looked set with fancy dishes I had never seen before.

My uncle, Matthew, met us there in a horse and buggy and he whipped the horses all the way to Hope, trying to get there before my grandmother died. She did recognize us but was gone in just a few minutes on December 28, 1908. My mother brought the younger boys home with us and put them in school at Richland. Dee was fifteen and Minor was twelve. Dee lived with Aunt Belle Brown, my grandfather's sister, some of the time.

My grandparents, David and Sarah Hall, moved from Richland Springs, Texas, to Hope, New Mexico, and bought land to farm on. I can't remember what they grew, but did well.

My mother's sister, Essie, married while in Hope to Robert Cole. She died not long after of appendicitis.

My grandmother hurt her hand while in Hope. I can't remember how, but she couldn't finish her book, so I wanted to fill in with what little I can remember. I am ninety-four years old now and was only nine when she died, so I can't contribute much.

BEULAH MABLE LAMBERT

I am the daughter of James Mathias Hall, the eldest of "Diddin's" sons. I have always had an affinity towards this grandmother I never knew. We were taught to call her Mama Hall and love her memory and to hold her in the highest respect.

Some of the things I am writing about are the incidents told to me by my father. According to him, his mother had a very hard life. She was very small in stature, (Daddy said) he bet she only weighed eighty or ninety pounds upon her death. She bore many children and at times worked the fields to provide food for her children. Her husband seemed to be away from home a lot. These are the names of her children. Amy (Hall) Warren, who had one child, Beulah; Essie Hall, who had no children, James M. Hall, who had two children, and Little Myrtle, who was a midget and died while still a child. Aunt Amy said she remembered Little Myrtle could walk under the dining room table while she was standing straight up, at this time she was about six years of age.

My mother (Odessa Skaggs Hall) said she had seen one of the little girl's dresses, and she held her hands about fifteen to twenty inches apart to show the length of the dress. Burney Hall, who had five children; two boys and three girls. Uncle Dee Hall, who had one daughter. Uncle Minor Hall, who remained single until his death leaving no heirs.

When she married, my other grandmother Martha Ellen (Hutchison) Skaggs said that her mother helped to make Mama Hall's wedding dress and when my Grandmother Skaggs married, Mama Hall helped make her wedding dress. Mama Skaggs knew her well and told me that Mama Hall was very well respected in the area. Mama Skaggs said she never heard an unkind word about Mama Hall. She said Mama Hall was a wonderful musician and played for all the dances until she got religion.

Mama Hall was given a gift of knowing things happening to her family even though it might be miles away. One instance Daddy told me about was when she was on her death bed, she looked up at her daughter Essie, took her hand, and said, "Essie, Essie you poor girl you won't be alive a year from now." (Essie was a healthy young woman, recently married.) Shortly after this and Mama Hall's death, Essie became sick. Her husband took her to a doctor and he diagnosed appendicitis. She went on to a hospital in another town, which I think was Almagorda. They went in a horse drawn buggy. He left her there after the operation, he visited several times. The last time the doctor told him he could take her home the next time he came for a visit. When he returned he came prepared to take her home, only to find that she had died suddenly. In those days the cause was unknown; today we would blame a blood clot. Mama Hall at this same time turned to my father, who was a young bachelor, and told him, "Mathy, you won't settle down until you marry. The woman you marry will be a good business woman and because of her you will be alright. You will marry late and have two children. The first child will be a boy who will marry young and die young. He will give you lots of worry. Your second child will be a girl who will bring fame and honor to the family name." My dad did not marry until after his thirtieth birthday. My mother was a business woman having a millinery shop in town. The first year they had a boy. Ray was a handsome man who was married and divorced; he died by his twenty-fourth birthday in the U.S. Army in Bataan just before Bataan fell in World War II. Ray was helpless to control his drinking and as we now know was an alcoholic. Had he lived he might have found help today.

I am the other child she spoke of. I was born in 1927 after they had been married ten years. I certainly have not gained fame nor have I gained wealth. I like to think that Mama Hall would be pleased with me as I have earned a master of arts degree under great hardships. I've always felt I was doing this partly to please her. I have also become a Christian, which I feel she would have approved of. I have received her gift of knowing when things are going to happen. I do not know explicit details as she did, I only have premonition.

Daddy said Mama Hall held education in a high esteem, and she told him she hoped her book would sell so her children could obtain a education.

Mama Hall must have had a great sense of humor. I remember Daddy telling a funny story about his taking the horses to pasture. It seems he had to pass a cemetery going and coming. When he was going (riding a horse and guiding the others) he would put his hand to the side of his face, on the cemetery side so he could not see the cemetery. Going back on foot, he would place the other hand up to shade his vision of the cemetery. One night Mama Hall and Aunt Amy decided to scare him. They put a sheet around a broom stick and a pillow case over the straw part; on the pillow case they drew a face. It must not have been dark yet because he could see the "broom man" when his mother and sister raised it up. As he came to the cemetery on the way back, they raised up the broom and moaned *"whooo-whooo."* Daddy said he was so scared that he cut and ran as fast as he could. He said "I damned near killed my fool self. I must have ran over and through more than one barbed wire fence." He said when his mother and sister got home they doubled up laughing at him, but when they saw him all bloody and hurting they felt sorry for what they had done.

One interesting story Daddy told was when they were all at home, seems they lived in a certain house, maybe one room or two, in a certain area of land. At regular intervals on the same day of the month three loud claps of noise such as a heavy chain banging struck three times, then all was quiet. They would wait to see what they could find out. They always heard the noise but saw nothing. This was always in the early evenings. The family decided to move the building to another site. They cut small logs, and would roll the house upon these logs, as one log came free at the back the free log would be moved to the front of the building, placed under it, and the house would roll onto it as it passed over it. On the day it was to be moved, when they jacked the building up to place the first logs under it, they all heard three loud knocks with a chain. This was in the middle of the day and the only time they heard it in daylight and last time they heard this noise.

I was privileged to know two or three of Mama Hall's brothers. One, I believe his name was Joe, came to visit Daddy. He was the sheriff of San Saba County, Texas. I was very young, but I remember a great tall man, who I was afraid of. Much later after I was grown and married, my husband and I drove my dad to Carlsbad, New Mexico, to see his Uncle Dee Harkey. What a picturesque little man. He was as small as Mama Hall was. He had just had his book on the Lincoln County War and his life published. He was so sweet to me; he got me a copy of *Mean As Hell* and autographed it for me. He was sheriff of Lincoln County, New Mexico, after Pat Garrett. They were close friends and both of them knew Billy the Kid.

After Daddy talked to Uncle Dee he remembered it was Mama Hall (Diden) who climbed the tree to escape the Indians when she was a girl. He had reported in his book that another sister had climbed the tree. He said Mama Hall had jumped into the creek and almost drowned to escape the Indians. After he and Daddy talked he remembered that it was Mama Hall (Diden) who had climbed the tree. Uncle Dee remembered when his sister died that the children were scattered. The older ones went out on their own and the younger ones went to live with relatives. One brother went to live with Aunt Amy and one (perhaps this was the same one) lived with an aunt Bell (Hall) Brown. I think Uncle Dee had one live with him for awhile. Papa Hall sold the home and went to take "baths" at the hot springs as he had been reported to have asthma.

Aunt Amy kept her mother's book for many years. One day my dad asked Aunt Amy to let him read "mama's book." Aunt Amy told him to keep it and for him to try to finish it. She said, "I guess I'll never do anything with it." Daddy kept the book and when I married he gave her most prized possession to me, and told me to finish it if I could. I rented a safety deposit box to keep it safe (at times I could hardly afford to eat, but I kept that box). I went to Uncle Burney, Uncle Dee, Uncle Minor and also my dad, talked to them and made notes to try and finish this book. I also talked to Beulah, who is Aunt Amy's daughter, and since she was the only one of us to see and remember Mama Hall I was particularly interested in her comments. She will be writing her own memories so I will not attempt to render her additions.

One day Maridell (Beulah's daughter) and her mother came to visit me. I had approached my daughter Amy Anne Haaland about passing this book down my daddy's line and she told me to go ahead and pass it down to Beulah's line as she was not interested in it and did not want to take care of it. With an aching heart I realized it was time to pass the book on down. With tears in my eyes I handed Beulah Mama Hall's book and she in turn handed the book to Maridell. I made a stipulation that she purchase a fireproof box to keep the book in. I went to town with Maridell when she bought the fireproof box. She bought one that just fit the manuscript. Maridell married very young and her daughters are interested in family history. Her daughters will carry these writings and Mama Hall's dream on down the family line. Maridell is having this book published and it gives me great joy, although a lump forms in my throat when I realize I can no longer hold these treasured pages in my hand. Maridell has great-grandchildren now and I can envision many young people seated around as the previous generation reads these prized words.

With enormous gratitude to you Sarah (Harkey) Hall, I thank you and I remain your granddaughter.

AMY ELLEN (HALL) HAALAND

Sarah Harkey Hall

Introduction

Few accounts of life in nineteenth-century Texas provide either the vivid personal detail or the poignancy of these recollections set down by Sarah Harkey Hall in 1905. Her narrative, written at age forty-eight for her children, captures the rhythms of daily and seasonal life in frontier San Saba County and chronicles her struggle for physical and emotional survival, as well as the struggles of her family and her community. Unlike many pioneer memoirs written for later generations, Sarah's does not assume a nostalgic or triumphant tone and does not glide over the daily hardships of life in a new country. The result is a remarkable record of frontier endurance, a record more bitter than sweet.

As Sarah states, her parents and older siblings settled in 1853 or 1854 on Richland Creek in Central Texas, within the then-vast boundaries of Bexar County. They were among the first westering immigrants in the region, locating "one mile east of Richland Springs among the recently vacated wigwams of the Comanche Indians." The community of Richland Springs apparently did not yet exist, and San Saba County would not be carved from Bexar County until 1856.[1]

Sarah, the fifth child, was born on the family homestead on March 2, 1857. Joseph M. (Joe), Nancy Jane (Jane), Julia, and John A. had preceded her, and her mother would bear eight more children in the next twelve years: James T. (Jim), Levi J., Martha E., Jefferson D. (Jeff), Polly Ann (Annie), Daniel Riley (Dee), Moses I. (Mose), and Eli L. In 1869, after giving birth prematurely to Eli, Sarah's mother died. Her father, who had been in declining health, passed away three weeks later. His dying wish was that the children, under the leadership of the eldest, seventeen-year-old Joe, remain together on the farm, with the exception of the newborn Eli, who was temporarily sent to an aunt's.

Between 1869 and 1875, Sarah saw her two older sisters marry and move to nearby homesteads. Joe, unable to support the family by remaining on the farm, worked as a Texas Ranger and at other jobs that kept him away from home in order to obtain money, while John proved good-hearted but irresponsible. Joe sometimes sent money, and oldest sister Jane took in Martha and Jim, but Sarah was responsible for most of her younger siblings most of the time.

Sarah herself married Dave Hall in October 1875; they would remain in the Richland Springs area, moving from farm to farm.[2] With Sarah's marriage — and Joe's soon thereafter — the younger children shifted about among their married siblings. Sarah's first pregnancy ended in miscarriage.[3] She had a baby boy in January 1877, but he died that March. A second child, Amy, was born in March 1879. Essie May arrived in March 1882, James Mathias in 1885, and Myrtle in December 1887. Throughout these busy years, Sarah suffered from poor health. She also suffered the violent deaths of three of her brothers: John in 1878, Jim in 1880, and Mose in 1888.

Sarah's narrative focuses on her childhood and early married life, speeding up after 1880 and, although she had planned to carry the account further, ending with Mose's death.

Sarah knew how to have fun — to play practical jokes and enjoy dances — and acknowledged the good she found in others, but for the most part, the tone of the narrative is somber and sad. Sarah describes her birthplace as "where I first saw the light of this unfriendly world," and she frankly outlines how fear, worry, and melancholy infused her childhood, adolescence, and early marriage — "by nature, I inherited all caution and care." Sometimes the tone seems self-pitying, as when Sarah looks back on herself as a child, "pale face and frail form with matted hair and tattered garments . . . half clothed and barefooted, shivering in the cold." But her circumstances were often indeed grim, and her sympathies extended to her siblings and to anyone needing a hand. A sensitive soul, she vowed after her early experiences, "If it is possible to help [anyone in distress], I certainly will."

Sarah certainly saw and experienced enough distress. She

adored her father — "My heart was full of joy when he was near" — but watched him die a slow, painful death over a period of four years. She recognized that her overworked, ever-pregnant mother had a hard lot, but Sarah nonetheless suffered greatly from her mother's harshness and apparent lack of patience and love. Deprived of both parents shortly after her twelfth birthday, she soon bore full responsibility for a horde of younger siblings. She watched the family begin to fragment, struggled to maintain the proprieties of young womanhood without an adult's guidance, began having health problems, then entered into a troubled marriage. Dave Hall was kind to her siblings and eventually proved to be a good provider, but her honest assessment of his failings as a husband, including occasional drinking sprees, shows that the two were ill-matched in many ways.

These personal circumstances often made a number of already-hard frontier realities even harder. Whatever one's situation, in the San Saba County of which Sarah writes, settlers faced a number of substantial frontier challenges, chief among them the continuing threat of Indian attack, the unremitting labor required to maintain a frontier homestead and achieve or maintain a decent standard of living, lack of educational opportunities and medical care, and a fluid and sometimes troubled frontier community.

All of these challenges are amply represented in Sarah's narrative. Fear of Indians pervaded her childhood, and she writes of "sitting up at night listening to the whistle of the Comanches all around and shivering with fear and trembling." While Indian "bogeymen" were more myth than reality on some parts of the American frontier, Sarah had every reason to be fearful; neighbors were regularly killed or captured by the still-strong and defiant Comanches. When these raiders took advantage of Texas involvement in the Civil War to step up harassment of the western frontier, the Harkeys temporarily lost valuable neighbors who moved to a safer location in Bell County.

In 1869, shortly after the elder Harkeys' deaths, depredating Comanches led the children to move in with two of the other families on Richland Creek in classic "forting up" fashion, and neighbors on the San Saba River soon sent wagons and teams to move all three families to their settlement. Joe and John traveled back and forth to cultivate the farm fields, then, tiring of the trouble, moved the family home in the fall — "not a neighbor nearer than the San Saba River."

Sarah endured a number of Indian frights and had her pony stolen by Indians but still responded with horror to a graphic account Joe, then a Texas Ranger, gave her in 1873 concerning the "fine sport" his company had in running down and scalping a small band.

Whether hostile Indians were in the area or not, families still had to go on with the myriad outdoor chores, which for the Harkeys included hunting and home-building, planting and harvesting, damming and irrigating, stockraising, hog-butchering, molasses-making, fodder-hauling, and pecan-gathering. While most of these were activities performed by adult and adolescent males, the younger children also participated in some, particularly the pecan-gathering, and Sarah planted corn seeds until she felt "as if I was cut in two just above the hips." Meanwhile, her mother and her older sisters — and eventually Sarah — were making soap, gardening, and no doubt doing laundry outside, while inside they were spinning, weaving, sewing, and making candles.

In short, the Harkey home, like most of its frontier neighbors', represented the old preindustrial home-as-factory. "We never had to buy anything," Sarah writes. The price for this self-sufficiency in a frontier family of fifteen, however, was constant work, constant struggle, constant fear of running out. All of this was understandably exacerbated for Sarah by her parents' deaths and the overwhelming responsibilities that followed for her. Sometimes she and the younger siblings were without food and clothing as winter approached, and it was left to her to find a way to meet the crisis.

Sarah showed great ingenuity in stretching her scanty resources, but how serious was the challenge is reflected in the fact that she gained as much peace of mind from having everyone "fairly well clothed" as she did from the gradual diminishing of the Indian threat. Meanwhile, the unending effort clearly took its toll on her physical and emotional health.[4]

In Sarah's narrative, we do see the movement away from full home production. When the family could, it bought material and even ready-made clothing, and these items seemed a godsend to young women who had processed clothing from fiber to cloth to apparel. Still, the home factory was far from disappearing on the

West Texas frontier in the 1870s and 1880s. As an adolescent and young married woman, Sarah farmed as much as her health permitted, quilted, made sausage, spun and knitted, kept bees, sheep, hogs, and geese. Her self-sufficiency is apparent in her remark to a younger sister about 1880: "Annie, let's go over in Jim's field and plant some cotton to make us some mattresses."

Sarah had delighted in learning such skills — "I always had a great desire to know how to do all domestic work" — but her delight in book-learning could not be equally well developed. Her parents clearly valued learning, and her father home-schooled the four older children and began teaching Sarah. After his death, Sarah periodically managed to attend a frontier school, but the opportunities were limited, the school terms only three months a year. She obviously took pride in her ability to catch up with and surpass more fortunate scholars, but never saw any educational future, given her responsibilities and lack of finances. "I always regretted that I hadn't the opportunity for an education," she would write in 1905. "I craved book knowledge, and do yet."

Medical services were as limited as educational opportunities on the frontier, sometimes with disturbing results; Sarah complained that her father had only "quacks" to treat him as his health deteriorated. But her account — in particular, the incident in which she was drained of poison from a rabid skunk bite by a borrowed "mad stone" — contains fascinating material on frontier folk-healing practices during a time when settlers knew they would have to take responsibility for their own healing and did so.

In most cases of injury and illness, the far-flung frontier community pitched in to help. Sarah remembered with gratitude the neighbors' assistance with her ill father and a neighbor's attendance on her when she was ill. Neighbors also taught the girls sewing skills, saw to the children's safety when Indians were raiding, and provided fun and pleasure with singing schools, dances, and Christmas celebrations.

At the same time, however, any sense of community was undermined by the continuing physical isolation of homesteads such as the Harkeys', by the daily labor demands each family faced, and by the shifts in population as some settlers gave up and backtracked while others moved on.

Such factors contributed to Sarah's feeling that frontier neighbors let her down. Left alone with her younger siblings, all of them sick, she felt abandoned, and years later wrote ominously, "Everyone was too busy to minister to our needs, but there is a time coming when everyone of those people will have to answer to this accusation."

The frontier community also proved ineffectual, indifferent, or actively hostile in other ways, as exemplified by the death of Sarah's brother John in a dispute over a horse-thievery charge. John was scheduled to testify against the man who shot him, and the charges of horse-thieving had apparently split the people of the Richland Springs area into suspicious factions. John's murder — and the later murders of Jim and Mose in quarrels and misunderstandings at other West Texas locations — fall into a pattern of lawless feuding apparent in Texas in the decades after the Civil War. In San Saba County in particular, tensions built in the 1870s and erupted in the 1880s.[5]

Although Sarah did not plan to end her manuscript with Mose's death, it is perhaps appropriate that she did so, for the ending says much about the ways in which Sarah took comfort from a hard life and endured. In many ways, Sarah's narrative supports the bleak interpretation of the frontier experience provided by "new western historians," in which the hardships of the frontier overcome and shatter families.[6] Old hurts and old failures in living together do thread through Sarah's narrative, but so does a strong love of her family, a strong longing for familial wholeness, and with it a desire for faith and meaning for herself and her loved ones. These longings are greatly assuaged for Sarah by Mose's dying words, "Mother has come after me . . . Oh, what a shield I have now." Sarah's narrative exposes the pain and struggle of a hard-pressed frontier family but sustains a note of hope and amply illustrates her theme of fortitude in the face of life's disappointments, large and small.

PAULA MITCHELL MARKS, PH.D.

xviii

1. The entry for Richland Springs in the *Handbook of Texas* (Texas State Historical Association, 1952) notes that the community "was settled as early as 1855."

2. In the narrative, Sarah clearly gives her birthdate as March 2, 1857, and her date of marriage as October 3, 1875, yet she notes that she was twenty years old when she wed. Family records show the dates to be correct, so one can only assume she misstated her age.

3. Sarah simply used the term "abortion," but clearly meant a spontaneous abortion, or miscarriage, as she cited an illness leading to the loss.

4. For a narrative similar to Sarah's in depicting the effects of a fragmenting family life and constant toil, see Matilda Doebbler Gruen Wagner's account of her life in Jo Ella Powell Exley's *Texas Tears and Texas Sunshine* (Texas A&M University Press, 1985), pp. 107–123.

5. See C. L. Sonnichsen's *I'll Die Before I Run* (University of Nebraska Press, 1988 ed.)

6. For example, see Lillian Schlissel, Byrd Gibbens, and Elizabeth Hampsten, *Far From Home: Families of the Westward Journey* (Schocken Books, 1989).

Essie, Sarah, Amy (standing), Matthew, and Dave Hall.

Chapter 1

Born in a Perilous Time

I HOPE MY READER will not think my story absurd or incredible. What I am going to write is real facts of my life up to the present year, 1905. I write this for the benefit of my children; that they may realize the benefit of patience and endurance.

My ancestors were of fine descent. My father was quarter German; my mother was an English lady, born in West Virginia. My father was born in North Carolina. They moved to Texas in the year of 1853 or 1854 and located in San Saba County in the valley of Richland Creek, one mile east of Richland Springs among the recently vacated wigwams of the Comanche Indians. This was the spot where I first saw the light of this unfriendly world on March 2, 1857. When I reflect back to my extreme early childhood, I behold those lovely grandeurs of valleys and glades, all covered with fine mesquite grass, and behold the scattered live oak trees clothed in their evergreen, and the mesquites here and there and the great herds of fat cattle, deer, and buffalo rushing down the glades to water, it seems almost a thousand years ago.

Here among the cruel tribe of the Comanche Indians, my father settled with my mother and four children; two brothers and two sisters, older than myself. He erected a log cabin, bought 160 acres of land with one near neighbor; always expecting an attack by Indians. He toiled late and early. Oftentimes, when he

1

knew the Indians were all around, he would wait until after dark and take his team and Mother and the little ones and slip to his near neighbor. On his way there, he would hide his team in a close thicket which he had selected for this purpose. They would often keep watch all night with the little ones shivering with fear, thinking every move an approach of Indians.

I was born in this perilous time and, by nature, I inherited all caution and care. My first recollection is of fear of Indians; sitting up at night listening to the whistle of the Comanches all around and shivering with fear and trembling. We were taught never to get but a short distance from our little hut, for it was no uncommon thing to get news of some family being massacred in the most horrible and cruel manner, with the capture of the women, and perhaps some little innocent girl being carried off with them. At the same time they would have the scalp of father and brothers to present to the captives and if they showed any grief, their torture was only increased until relieved by death. We would often venture out to the old vacated wigwams to gather trinkets left by the Indians; beads and such like. We always had strand after strand of them, which our childish hearts enjoyed. Although, once we were missed by our parents, we would hear the call, "Come here children, you will be picked up by the Indians," then we would take to our heels.

My father soon put in a farm and began to try to farm with poor success, but never an entire failure. He always raised something. Although, in those early days that country was very droughty. My father was very intelligent and full of energy; killed game, such as bear, deer, antelope, and turkey. We had plenty of meat always. He would dress the deer skins and my mother would make coats and pants of those dressed hides for my brothers, and would sometimes make whole suits for men and sell them. When my brothers' pants would wear out over the knees, she would re-cover that part with a new piece of buckskin, which she called "foxing their britches." My father bought a couple of milk cows and a few sheep and from this sheep wool my mother carded and spun thread and wove cloth for all necessary uses.

My earliest recollection was the fear of Indians and trying to catch the sunshine through the cracks of our little log cabin, and the horror I felt to the humming of the spinning wheel. My parents were both very industrious; always had something for every child to do. My oldest brother was a great help to my father. When he was eight years old he could plow, chop, and drive oxen well. He was very manly. My father was very punctual in every respect. In a few years, the few neighbors were in need of a schoolteacher, and my father was employed as their teacher. He was a poor man, but with patience and endurance, he prospered fast. He was a wood workman and a cooper. He could apply himself anyway he wished; was so jovial and kind and full of life, everyone was his friend. He was a very small man in stature, but I thought him the greatest man on earth. I really loved him better than I loved my mother.

I always thought my mother was not as kind to me as I wished her to be. I was a very frail, delicate child; full of sympathy for everything and everybody. My father always doted on me and favored me in everything. My mother was not so patient, was fretful, but now I can realize her condition. Her children were like stairsteps and such a burden to card and spin and weave every thread. We all wove and made our clothes by hand. No wonder I thought her impatient. My oldest sister soon became a great help to her; could spin filling *[sic]* at eight years old.

I was the baby nurse. Oh! the hum of the wheel and the rattle of the cards made me weary. I knew my long weary day had begun sitting by the cradle; rock, rock all the long summer days. So sleepy I would get, I would fall over asleep but was soon awakened with a button willow switch. I thought the baby awfully cross. My father made me a nice little chair to nurse in. I would take the little brother up and rock him until I was so tired. I moved up close to the fire with him, but he cried the more. Finally my mother took him and he still cried. She began to examine him to find the cause of his fretfulness and I had blistered the poor little fellow's feet on the bottom where I had rocked over the fire. I was too small to discern his feet over the coals of fire. I was so sorry I could have shed tears, but my mother scolded me severely. I never did any wrong on purpose. I always told the truth about everything, although my mother punished me often when I was innocent.

She taught my older brother, then me, myself, our ABC's while carding. I learned faster than him and I would run to the workshop to where my father was always employed to tell him my progress. He would dote on me. Oh, my heart would leap in my bosom for joy. This was before I was old enough to be nurse. I stayed with him in the shop. I would assist him in many ways; would turn the turnlay *[sic]* for him to shape up nice pieces of furniture, and turn the grindstone to sharpen his bits. I learned by observation to sharpen all kinds of tools, yet I was very young.

Chapter 2

The Erection of Our New House

IN THOSE DAYS EVERYBODY lived in log huts floored with puncheon or slabs, dressed on one side with a briad ax, and covered with boards made by hand; would saw their timber with a crosscut saw in any length they wished to have the boards. Then with a froe *[sic]* they split the boards; never used nails to fasten the roof as we do now. They laid the boards on by layers clear across the top of the house, then weighed them with a log at the top and bottom and so on until the house was covered.

As I've already told you, my parents prospered with their rough commodities. Now, they had a nice bunch of cattle, though small, and sheep, hogs, goats and a few head of horses [my father] had raised from one brood mare which he kept locked in stables every night from the Indians. My mother had a flock of geese which gave the very small children employment to keep those geese, which was a task. They loved mesquite beans and when once they got to running after them, it was a task to turn them back.

My father's success enabled him to erect a better house. As the country slowly developed, there were more conveniences. There was a sawmill erected on the San Saba River and plenty of timber for sawstock *[sic]* of elm and post oak so he cut and hauled timber with his ox team to the mill and had lumber sawed to build a frame house. In the summer of 1861 he completed the frame house. Now, as you will see from the dates given, I was four years old. My mother raised fine beets that spring. I would go with her to her garden after those nice beets. I longed to see her place them on the table to serve, for I did relish nice pickled beets. I would gather the fallen nails my father and Mr. Gunter, the hired hand, dropped. In the fall he built a chimney to the house and on the top stone he cut the date of the building on it, so I know I am not mistaken in my age at that time. Our new residence was the most important building in all the county. He cut two small windows, twelve by fourteen inches, in the south and north with plank shutters.

My father felt that his family was safer now when he had to make a chase after the Indians, which was often. Every man in the surrounding county went except guards left to defend the women and children. The Indians would rush in and take every horse possible and kill and scalp someone, capture some woman or little girl, or, likely, massacre a whole family. Then all the citizens collected in a rush and started on their trail. Sometimes they would recapture the horses but seldom recaptured the women and children.

I well remember one raid when they killed one of our neighbors and scalped him and cut and slashed his body in the most horrible manner. Oh, such a terrible scene for innocent women and children to gaze upon; enough to almost chill the blood of anyone with a conscience. It was the first corpse my eyes ever looked upon, and it is still fresh in my mind. The citizens rushed off in pursuit and in several days came upon the Indians, made their charge, and they scattered in every direction. One very large Indian was chased so close he took to a thicket. The citizens surrounded the thicket and watched their chance to put in good shots. He could talk a little English and would say, "Indian won't kill poor white man in thicket, don't kill poor Indian in thicket." One neighbor was crawling in the thicket to get near him when, instantly, an arrow zipped and the spike struck his forehead and struck the skull and doubled up. They closed in on him and then killed him. He was their chief and was wearing plaits of some white lady's hair, decorated with beads. They scalped him and brought his scalp in. All the rest made their escape. We now had one neighbor above us on the creek and one below us.

My father would raise wheat and corn, more or less every year, and provided the best he could for his family. My oldest brother now began to do quite a good deal of farm work while my father was continually busy in his shop making wheels, reels, warping bars and looms for manufacturing cloth.

As the children increased to my parents, the more labor was increased. When night came on, we knew our tasks were at hand. Our light consisted of dogwood sticks my brother, older than me, and myself would bring in every eve. Then we had to pick wool until late. Mother would kust *[sic]* or card, father would teach my older brother and two older sisters, and all us smaller ones picked wool. He always rose early; everyone to work by sunrise. As our brain and strength enlarged, our labor increased. Every year he found us more helpful to him.

When I was very young, he put me to dropping corn. He went one round with me, showed me how to step to drop it regular, then went about his work. I was ever after the corn dropper. My oldest brother laid off the rows, I dropped the seed, my next older brother covered it. I have gone to bed oftentimes and felt as if I was cut in two just above the hips, that part cast away. I could sleep. I never complained, though I never saw a well day. My father was very kind to me; never scolded or whipped me.

All through the summer our time was employed, not a minute to lose, preparing for winter. Often Mother would sew late hours at night and then some of us children would suffer with cold before she could possibly clothe us. Father made our shoes, if we had any at all. He taught us by the fire on cold winter nights, after all preparations were made for winter. I learned very fast; soon could read well and was studying a reader called *The Texas Reader*. Some beautiful pieces were in it. I had good understanding for a little child. I would become absorbed in some of the reading, I would break forth in sobs.

I always knew my lesson and was anxious to hear Father call, "Come, Sarah, recite your lesson." I was born with the gift of the reading the expression of the eye. I could see in his expression he was so delighted with me. My heart was full of joy when he was near. Mother tried to teach me to spin, and it seemed impossible. I would try my best, but I feared her and I would get nervous and I could not learn. My father watched awhile and said, "Mother, I'll teach Sarah to spin." Oh, how my heart leaped for joy. He took hold of my hand at the spindle and my right hand on the rim of the spinning wheel and in twenty minutes I could draw out a thread. I was of a temperament that I could not bear to be scolded, and was amiable in everything I tried to do. I wanted to be loved, not chastised. My two older sisters would envy me, called me "Father's little lady." It would grieve me for them to talk to me so. I was too young to know he was really partial to me.

He enjoyed vocal music so much and understood rudiments of music and every Sunday morning he had singing. Mother was a fine singer. While neither one was in the church, they were both very moral and taught their children to be moral. I don't remember ever being at church, but twice, until I was fourteen years old. Once I remember being at a camp meeting, it seems. I don't know how old I was; then again at a funeral of a home boy. They never had any preaching, but the few neighbors loved each other with brotherly love and kindness; never had any hardness whatever. They took a great interest in each other's welfare; all united in love toward each other and would neighbor fifteen or twenty miles, but always had several escorts. They never went alone and a spy always went ahead.

Chapter 3

My Father and Mother's Conversion

NOW, AS I'VE ALREADY told you, my parents were very moral in all things, yet never had obeyed the gospel. Mother leaned toward the Methodist doctrine and, of course, thought that the only way. If Father had any choice in churches, I have no remembrance of it. He always had his fun with us children and everyone that he came in contact with.

Finally, there came a new kind of preacher along; was now over on the San Saba River. He was very wonderful, insomuch that his doctrine went abroad everywhere. So they concluded to go over and hear what this great man taught. They took escorts and went over. Father became so interested, he wasn't ready to go home at the appointed time, but Mother was so completely disgusted with the doctrine and unnerved from uneasiness over her little ones at home, she got escorts and came home. We were watching and waiting their return and ran to meet them, when, to our surprise, Father was not with her. We all cried out, "Where is Father?"

Her reply was, "He has gone to Jerusalem."

"Oh, where is Jerusalem, Mother?" for we had never heard of such a place before. She told us then that he stayed with the old preacher. She wasn't in the best humor, either. He stayed a few days longer and when he came home he talked a great deal of the new doctrine, but she couldn't endure the thoughts of it. Father had the preacher promise to visit him at an appointed time and told her he would come at that time. "No, he won't, either," she said. "I wouldn't listen to such stuff as he preaches. You surely have lost your mind to be carried off with such doctrine as that." But he came and Father had our neighbor's family come in and he preached several days at our home. Mother would leave the room; wouldn't listen at all. Father soon caught the seed sown into his heart and made the good confession and was baptized. The preacher departed, but was a constant visitor of Father's, and always preached when he came.

Soon our neighbor made the confession and was baptized. This was something new to me to see a man take people into the water and dunk them. So Father always read the scripture day after day and, after so long, got Mother's attention and the next visit of the preacher's, she made the confession and was baptized. She was a very large lady and when he went to baptize her I thought, "He never can get her up, she will drown," but he lifted her with ease. Then Father taught the more, dividing the word and marking it as he read from Genesis to Revelation.

So many times childish ideas would arise in my mind. I wished to ask questions concerning the resurrection of the dead. I will relate one instance. I heard his reading of the first resurrection, and the grown hogs had overlain a little pig the night before. How I did want to ask him if it would be resurrected before me, as it died first. That one thought bore on my mind for several days, but he always taught me to listen, to learn, and not ask questions. I was young; don't know just my age at that time, but the word of the Lord was sown in my heart through the preaching of my father at home. I always carried his Bible to him when he sat down to rest and carried it back to the desk when he finished reading. That dear old Book is now in my possession. I often take it and read from the references his blessed hand had marked out for me years ago and, oh, what a pleasure it often has given me.

I never remember spending idle days. He always had employment for me and all the children. When he began making molasses, I carried a small hatchet and a little block and cut the heads off the cane after it was stripped of the fodder and cut down, which was not hard work. Nothing ever seemed hard to me that he told me to do. When the fodder was to be hauled out, which had to be done very early of mornings, I helped carry it to the fence where it would be convenient to get to. I would begin long before daylight and work until breakfast, eat my breakfast, wash the dishes next, then care for the baby until dishwashing again. Somehow I was very unfortunate about breaking dishes. It seemed like every time I washed dishes, I broke a piece. I never will forget one Sunday morn I went to my dishwashing, as usual. I had a great large stack washed and stacked on a large, round, flat tin. I had the tin on a chair and all at once it became unbalanced and such a crash there was; just one plate and one cup and saucer left. Such a punishment I got. I never did forget it. Our neighbor, Mr. Brown, was there. He scolded Mother for punishing me so. That made it seem harder still to me.

We never had to buy anything. Father produced everything we used; raised his tobacco too. We had to worm every morn and when it matured, we cut it and let it lay until it took so much dew, then we brought it in and stemmed it and twisted it ready for the press. He made his press for that purpose. When he pressed it in the caddy, it was then put away for use. He also invented a wooden pump and had his tobacco patch near the water's edge and irrigated his tobacco. I remember once he sent me to worm the tobacco and I had seen the down leaves pulled and used in pipes to smoke, so I thought I would chew some. I pulled off a leaf and took a large chew of it. Oh my, I was the sick little girl. I never tried any more down leaves.

We were constantly busy at something, but were always on guard; always expecting to be picked up by the Comanches. When we started any place we went, we didn't have to be told to hurry, as children do now. I remember so well one raid the Indians made, striking in below where we lived, going across by churches, and capturing Elon Todd, a young girl. The mother had gone to warp a piece of cloth. Captain Todd went with her and took his little daughter up behind him. On their way to the neighbor's house, the Indians ran upon them. They started to run, but they captured Mrs. Todd instantly and Mr. Todd's horse began to pitch and threw his little daughter off and they captured her. They tortured Mrs. Todd so cruelly, scalping her by degrees, while yet alive. She took off her outside garments and gave them to the unmerciful cruels, but that only increased their cruel desire. She at last thought she would seem dead and so she lay perfectly still and lifeless and they left her for dead. When found soon after, she was alive. She lived twenty-four hours in such a condition. They carried her daughter off with them and kept her for years. Finally she was brought back, but she had got accustomed to their ways and was never satisfied with her people anymore. She had several children by the chief; said she loved her children and wanted to go to them.

Every occurrence like this would make us more cautious. I had seen the Indians rush horses up in the corners of Father's field fence and catch them. They lit on them in a hurry, for they knew they would be chased. In fifteen minutes there was a scout rushed in from the Colorado River, twelve miles north of Richland Creek. They gave them a hot chase, but never killed any. The Frontiers formed a company and kept out a scout all the time and by those means they were kept whipped farther west and their raids were only expected on light moons, which was a great relief to the frontier settlers. Now we could feel more safe. We could go to the head of the Springs and gather beads that would boil up with the beautiful white pebbles and the water so pure and clear.

When I reflect back to those days and behold the beautiful landscape of a gradual slope south, to the height of one hundred feet to the top of the hills, where so many times those redskins had tread the little paths to the cooling source of those springs, I can't help shuddering to see our danger; though I feel that the Lord has watched over me always.

Now, my father's health began to fail and had to depend on my two oldest brothers a great deal. He was putting in a dam to irrigate from the springs. The boys worked every spare day on the dam and I always carried their dinner to them when they worked. I would take it to the bluff and go along under the ledges which extended near where they worked, sometimes crawling up and peeping up on the level to see if I could see or hear anything, then drop back and continue my journey. Sometimes I would pick a handful of berries or pull a few plums, but any noise would make me start and I could hear my heart thump like horses feet, and often have wondered at having any mind at all. Those days are days never to be forgotten by me; they are stamped on my heart, never to be blotted out.

All our long summer days of toil were ended and all preparations were made for winter, which consisted of gathering sweet potatoes and pumpkins and holing them up, and hog killing, rendering out lard, then carrying water to run lye to make up soap for winter, which was a task that fell on the small children. It was one hopper of ashes after another. We had to drip until all the soap was made. By that time, Father had all a pair of shoes made who were entitled to them, and those were the oldest children. Mother had knit a pair of socks and stockings for each of them.

Then came our happiest days. We all had a bluebacked speller and reading of some kind, and Father would send us to the log hut to study. He gave us ample time to prepare our lessons, then began at the oldest to hear lessons and so on, until we had all recited. When recess came, we all made it convenient to play about the potato hills, and what a time we had eating raw potatoes and making cornstalk horses and riders.

When night came all had their chores to do and had to go after chaff for the oxen way across the field south of the house. It was an easy matter to go, but facing the bleak north winds coming back would almost chill me through. I remember one very cold morning he told me to drive the calves to the field on the north side of the creek. I turned them out and tried to drive them but, when they got opposite the house, they would turn their heads from the north wind and start back. My hands were so cold and stiff, I would run in to get warm. He would have me rub my hands in cold water and try again. I made the third try before I could get them to the creek, then one of them wouldn't cross. I picked up a small stone and threw it and struck it somewhere about the head and it dropped like it was shot and fell like it was pierced in the heart, but in a second or two it began floundering around and got up. Oh, how I was relieved and went on without any more trouble and put them in the field.

I always had a great desire to know how to do all domestic work. I watched Mother knit and knew in my mind that I could knit. I slipped out and selected two nice slim straws and then slipped out some yarn and began my experience of knitting. I threw on my stitches and proceeded to knit back and forth and soon knit. Oh, what a great accomplishment I had made in my childish mind, and I really had. I never had more than a change of clothing and when my frock became so tattered and torn, I would examine it closely to see if I could remedy it, that it would appear more neat. I soon saw by taking out the whole front and putting in a new one, it would be whole; but where was I to get the cloth? All had been consumed and not a piece left over. Then I felt so bad! My clothes had to last until spring until Mother could card and spin and weave cloth to reclothe me if they wore out. I had to do without. I remember once in the spring of the year, my second frock was completely worn out and my frock was compelled to be washed and Mother made me put on my father's shirt to have my dress washed. Before it was ready to wear, Captain Wood came to have my father to do some writing for him. Oh, how embarrassed I felt! I tried to shy his presence, but my little duties had to be performed without respect of my childish modesty. I can reflect back and behold my pale face and frail form with matted hair and tattered garments. A pitiful little creature I was with an envious heart to arise to the elevation of Queen Elizabeth, but woe to the path I have wed; always striving for right and never intending wrong. It almost breaks my heart to look upon a little helpless child, half clothed and barefooted, shivering in the cold.

Father gradually grew worse in health and was getting more unable to work; would seek every way to get along and provide for us. He invented a wine press and in 1863 there was a world of wild grapes. He had my two oldest brothers yoke the oxen and take the ox wagon and all us smallest children and go gather grapes to press. He sent us north, seven miles from home on a little creek called Wilbargo Creek. We found all the grapes we could gather. They pitched camp and went to work. He told us where to go at night. When night came, we went to the thicket where he had told us to go, and ate our supper and began to fix our pallets, when we looked out and saw him. He had gotten uneasy and came to see about us. He saw us safe in the thicket and went back home. We heard a bunch of wild hogs in the night grazing on acorns. We were frightened almost to death, for we thought them Indians. We lay perfectly still, not a word was said nor an eye closed for sleep. Next morning he came back to see if we were there; gave no instructions how to proceed with caution, and went back. We soon gathered a load and went home unharmed; pressed the wine and bottled it for sale. He sold every quart at seventy-five cents per quart.

He grew weaker every year and being way out on the frontier of Texas, it was impossible to get any medical aid of importance.

The quacks continually treated him, but he did not improve any. Now the Civil War had been in progress for nearly three years, but the frontier never suffered from it. Often the report was noised abroad that all the Union men would be forced to go. That caused Mother and we children great grief for Father was a Union man, but he strictly attended his own business and never was forced to go.

Chapter 4

Our Pecan Gathering

IN THE FALL OF 1864 there was a heavy crop of pecans and they were a good price, and Father never let an opportunity slip where there was any money. My oldest brother was now thirteen years old. Father had him to prepare the wagon and oxen and take the rest of the children and go to gathering pecans. He wasn't a good climber, he had such a fear of falling. Father went with us for a few days until he saw we proceeded all right, then he left it all to us. We worked late and early. Occasionally, he came to our camp to see how we were getting along. We gathered 350 bushels that fall and winter, but my, how I suffered with cold. I would pick up pecans day in and day out until at night, when I closed my eyes, I could see nothing but pecans.

When we gathered all the oxen could pull, we came home. Being accustomed to drinking wheat coffee in camp, which I never used at home, for milk was preferable, I had formed a great thirst for it. I went to the cupboard one day and Mother had a cup of ash lye sitting in there and, thinking it cold wheat coffee, I instantly seized it and took a swallow before I could discern what I had drunk. Oh, but if I didn't vomit. Forever after I examined what I drank before partaking.

Now, the pecans had to be marketed and prices were better at Brenham, Texas, and Father's health was such that my oldest brother had to market them, which brought a neat sum of money. Father made out a bill for supplies and dry goods; he bought 250 yards of calico and other goods. These were the first goods I ever saw purchased and now I had a real fine frock; a calico dress and so many nice articles our neighbors didn't have. Such beautiful goods, I was so delighted; so much nice sugar and lincon [sic] coffee. That is the way coffee was distinguished from wheat coffee.

Oh, we felt as if we had been set free instead of the negroes, but Father continued to grow worse. His voice was no longer heard singing hymns as he toiled in the shop and Mother would plead with him to not work so constant. With tear-dimmed eyes, often she would go to the shop and assist him and plead with him to take a rest, but to no avail. He was thoroughgoing and felt he couldn't lose the time. Mother still continued to make cloth and blankets, but was not in so great restraint all the time. He always had money and every dollar an honest dollar.

In those days there were thousands of unmarked and un-branded cattle from one to three years old. The majority of the early settlers marked and branded those cattle until they had large stocks and became immensely rich, but Father never branded one or allowed any branded for him. He always told his boys never to take anything that didn't belong to them. The cattle were not his. He knew his own, and wouldn't allow his brand put on one.

Now, Mr. Brown, our dear old neighbor, became very much dissatisfied with the depredating Indians and moved to Bell County. Oh, such grief it gave us to see them depart. That left one neighbor five miles above us and one five miles below, and Father so poorly. He could only work a few hours during the day in his shop, but kept everything going on in a business manner by my brothers. They were both very obedient and industrious. He continued to put in every spare day on the ditches and other improvements on the place. Our residence was located on the south side of the creek in a nice grove of beautiful elms. There were two very large elm trees just in front of the south door and such lovely shade they afforded in the heat of the summer. Father always took his rest there and read to us.

In the spring of 1865 he kept to his bed most all the time and no relief to be found until summer. He now got up again, but was never able to work anymore. He would give instructions to my brothers and they carried on his business. His appetite was ravenous, but his stomach wouldn't retain solid food. Mother always kept dainties prepared for him, such as his stomach could retain. She carried his meals to him where he set in the shade of those beautiful elm trees. Oh, how sad to see his pale face and thin form day after day growing worse and no relief to be found. If he only whistled a note or two, it put new life in Mother and all the children. She was so devoted to him. I can see her, in my childish grief, steal away from his presence and break forth in deep sobs of penetrating grief, which almost broke my heart, but gave her present relief. She would then wash her face and comb her hair before going to his presence again. She well knew the time was approaching, in the near future, when she would have to give up a most devoted husband and father. It was breaking her heart.

I was only in present grief. I waited patiently for his recovery and to hear him sing those beautiful hymns on Sabbath mornings, walking, and keeping time, and instructing his class of his own children, with Mother's clear, sweet voice carrying soprano. But, alas, four long years expired before he gained sweet relief. Four years of anxiety and grief to mother and children. I was ever near him to give him water. He was ever and anon in such agony of pain; never relieved only by that poisonous drug opium, which cost a great deal of money. He often sat in the shade as long as his strength would permit, then have a hard pallet made, often saying, "Mother, place rocks under my pallet. My pain is so great they will feel comfortable to me." He would lie down and toss from one side to the other, then raise in a sitting posture and pray God to relieve him by death and watch over his family with a protecting arm and shield them from danger and all evil temptations that might be thrown around them. Oh, I could hardly bear my grief. He had no rest day nor night and no assistants to help nurse him.

Once every few weeks, some of our relatives from San Saba River would come up and stay a few days. He was a man that wanted business going on. No one could relieve his pain and he couldn't entertain them unless they enjoyed the whole scriptures and but very few cared for the Gospel, so they would go back home. Now we had a neighbor living in the cabins deserted by Mr. Brown, a son-in-law of Mr. Brown, who is still living near my native home. They were constant friends of ours; always a friend in need.

The Indians were whipped to the far west by now. Their raids were not so often, but regular, every light moon. They came in and would steal horses, not often killing and scalping as in earlier days, but everyone kept on their guard. As they were whipped back, they drove the buffalo back with them, as they claimed them as their cattle. We, no more, saw many buffalo. Once in awhile, one would get off from its bunch and would take up with a bunch of cattle. A calf took up with our cattle and we kept it for a pet. We made one of the milk cows raise it and she became as fond of it as her own calf. It was great amusement to us to watch it go to the creek and wallow in the mud as a hog. When it was nine and a half years old, it took the fever. We treated it constantly, but to no avail. It continued to stay in the mud and water until it died. The cow continued to low for it for several days, which caused our grief for our beautiful pet to be more penetrating.

But our sorrowing for our buffalo was overcome by the great anxiety I had in the hope to see Father recover. I never once thought of any danger befalling Mother. She was so strong and healthy; never was sick, with the exception of nervous headaches once in awhile and that was only for a few hours and then was perfectly well again. But often she prayed to our merciful Father that if it was possible she had to give her most dearest of everything on earth, to be merciful unto her and grant her departure with him, that she would never know the pangs of grief caused by their separation by death. "Oh, merciful Father, watch over my little ones. I ask Thee to shield them from all harm and preserve their characters all through life, that they may present themselves honorable men and women." Oh, it seemed that all the world was sorrow and sadness to me now that Mother wanted to leave us alone in such a wild, unfriendly world, but when she presented a bright, cheerful face in Father's presence, my sadness vanished to a lighter degree; but I never felt truly happy as some children do. I was looking into the future, as young as I was. I never saw any real happiness for me, but trials and trouble awaiting me.

In the autumn of 1867, as the evenings began to get cool and pleasant, Father would sit or lie on his pallet under the shade of those beautiful elm trees in front of the door. I was sitting nearby him in my little chair when I heard a sentimental chirp of a bird on a limb over our heads, which gave me a presentiment of great sorrow that pierced my heart like an arrow. Father instantly arose and stepped on a chair and reached up and took hold of the little bird and said, "Here, Sarah, I will give it to you!" The little thing never fluttered or flounced with fear. I never saw any beauty in the little bird, while it was a real beautiful bird with a coat of green and a yellow collar. I held it in my hand. While my head was very heavy, never was there a caressing thought entered my mind toward the bird, while I had always loved the sweet little birds. After holding the beautiful little creature in my hand for some time, I looked down and it was dead. I prepared a grave and buried it nicely, but that chirp is clear in my mind until now. As the weather grew colder, he was confined to the house, which was very dull to him, besides all his miseries to endure through the long winter days and nights of severe cold.

In the month of December, the eleventh day, there was born another baby brother, which entitled me to the seventh brother and four sisters. The winter was severe with chilly, bleak storms of sleet and snow, driving all unprotected creatures before it. My evening duty was now a hard one. From abscesses on Mother's breast, she failed to give sufficient nourishment for the baby brother and I adopted goat's milk for his nourishment. Now, we had no milk goats, but our neighbor did. I set apart a certain goat for him. I went every evening and milked the goat. It became unruly for me to milk. The cold, chilly winds kept her adrift until I was compelled to make her fast and secure with a rope, which would detain me so long that my fingers would be almost stiff with cold. I would finish my task and hurry home that the milk could be prepared for his night's nourishment.

My oldest brother and sister had all the care of Father and Mother and the little babe and the overseeing of everything, which was a task, you may be sure. Father scarcely slept any and needed their watchful care to keep the room in a moderate temperature, which kept them up the greater portion of the night, keeping the fire recruited with wood, which was always prepared every evening for the night. Mother always molded her tallow candles in the fall for winter use. She had them stored away and when one would extinguish, they would replace a new one.

Mother was soon able to care for the babe; they both did

well. My little brother thrived on the milk and was soon the joy of our home. Father could no longer teach us in our studies. This was all left off, but the five oldest children could read and spell. Really, my oldest brother was a fair scholar; was a natural mathematician and grammarian, and his practical training gave him good qualifications to battle through the world. I was the fifth. I could read and write and spell fairly well, and had learned to make my letters with a stick on the ground and on the uppers of my shoes by looking at the copy in the first of my blueback speller. Father had us to commit to memory all the sentences in our speller, as far as we went, and I am so proud that he did. It laid a good foundation for an education, if I had been blessed with an opportunity; but, alas, my chance was past, all to my sorrow and grief.

Chapter 5

My Awful Fate

WHEN WELCOME SPRING BEGAN to show forth all her beauties of nature, my young heart should have been overjoyed with the beautiful flowers and the tender green foliage of the wide spreading elm trees and such a lovely stream just at our door on the north, all covered with green moss and cress near the edge, and the song of the brook as o'er the great shoals it rolled. I was only a sad-hearted little creature with blue eyes dimmed all spring and summer. Father kept to his bed, never arising only from the pangs of pain, with Mother watching over him with tear-dimmed eyes; not a ray of hope in her heart could rise, making eggnog and toddies and so many changes of dainties. With all her kind nursing and care of preparing diets, his stomach couldn't retain a mouthful and so hungry he was from morning till night. He was only a living skeleton. I never have seen an object living, so poor. The disease was so complicated that it was terrible to bear; dyspepsia, liver and kidney trouble, and rheumatism. He suffered intensely all through the spring and summer of 1868.

When winter set in the whole family was completely worn out and our neighbors were very kind to assist in nursing him. They would come by turns to assist through the nights. When spring began to peep forth again in 1869, Mother was expecting in a few months to be mother again and was very fond of salad greens, but had no garden vegetables. Wild greens were plentiful and Mrs. Duncan had a mess gathered for dinner. My brothers' dinners were prepared in a vessel and I was hurried to take my dinner and then carry their dinner to them where they were at work on the ditches at the head of the springs. When I came back, Mother was very sick and vomiting, with a severe pain in her stomach. It was Thursday. Mrs. Duncan stayed until late but, being exhausted from sitting up for several nights, she went home to rest and Mrs. Hall came to our assistance.

Mother grew worse. They sent a runner for the doctor, but he refused to come. He was an old quaint being and would send instructions how to treat the case. They had given so much Laudanum to annul the pain. She had fallen into a deep stupor, so that it became impossible to arouse her. We were kept out of the room to avoid her disturbance. All day Friday, at intervals, she would call me and I would run to her bedside and ask, "What do you want, Mother?" I would be told by the nurse, "Run on out. Your mother doesn't know what she is saying." I would gaze at her closed eyes and tremorous form, in wonder, for she was affected spasmodically by Laudanum. Friday evening late, she gave birth to a tiny baby brother, two months premature. Saturday, about noon, I saw my oldest brother lay her head off of his breast and lay it on the pillow and leave the room, whereupon, my uncle took his place and held her up. Oh, such struggles! I stood and watched her awhile and turned away. Walking out, I saw my brother was weeping. Oh, how sad I felt. Before the last ray had set, all her struggles had ceased. She was dead. I could not sleep. I would close my eyes, but would soon be started. I would think I heard her call me, but still in death she lay.

When the Sabbath sun arose we were all in a gloom of sorrow. There lay Mother's form so cold and Father on a pallet with a form so pale and deathly grim. "Oh God, have pity on the orphans," I pray. It was so great a shock to my tender heart, yet I could not realize the loss of a mother. Without a man to make her coffin near, they assisted Father to the workbench and he even had to oversee the pattern of her coffin. I left the house; could not bear to come near.

When all was made ready, I was called by my aunt. She asked me if I wanted to see Mother. I could not bear to look on her pale face in death. I only turned away. How often, oh how often, I have regretted not going, for her dear features left me forever. How often I've sat in the moonlight and waited the appearance of her spirit. I would sit and sob away my bitter grief, then dry away my tears and look, but lo, she was not there. I would often go and lean against the walls and listen in my imaginary mind and would hear her struggling for life.

After she was laid away, we returned home to Father and my aunt. She was left with him and the baby. She stayed a few days with us and then returned home to her family, and took the babe with her. Father knew he would soon go and leave us to the mercies of the world, to battle our way through life the best we could, but what time he had left he lost none in advising the oldest. I heard it all and it never departed from me. He instructed my two oldest sisters to preserve their characters above everything for, when once blotted, they were forever stained, never to be regained. Such beautiful petitions he sent to our Father in Heaven as our safeguard, and now I know there is everything in a fervent prayer. He tried to gain hope to get well. He had my oldest brother and sister to make ready to carry him to the Sulpher Springs in Lampasas County. They started and went as far as San Saba town. He met Doc Brocentour there and the doc persuaded him not to go. Brother carried him to Aunt's, where the little babe was, and Father said he was getting better and sent brother home to make ready for him to go to New Mexico for his health, and he would spend awhile with Aunt. My oldest sister stayed with him. Brother began making preparations for his trip; had been in the shop at work late and early for four days.

Mother had now been sleeping under the cold sod three weeks and I looked and saw eight or ten men coming and I saw a measuring reed on one of their shoulders, just like the one they had taken Mother's measure with. I ran to my sister and told her Father was dead. I looked again and they had gone to where brother was at work. He dropped everything and came to the house and told us Father was dead.

Then came my greatest grief. Oh, to think I had neither Father nor Mother. "Surely he isn't dead. I can't believe it. No, I shall look for him tomorrow." My childish hopes to see him on the morrow, as I had seen him go away, survived. All was sadness. My heart was heavy with suppressed grief, yet I longed to see the morning light.

They said he would be brought home tomorrow about twelve o'clock. I was in the kitchen all morning trying to get everything ready, my whole mind absorbed on seeing my father, with every cord of my heart almost bursting. I couldn't keep my mind on anything I would undertake to do. There was coffee to parch and it was now near eleven o'clock. I ran out and looked to see if they were in sight. I couldn't see any sign of the approaching procession. I went back to the kitchen, got my coffee to parching and in a few minutes I heard one of the small children say, "I see Papa coming." I dropped everything and ran to see, expecting to see his pale face and thin, frail form of which I was anxiously awaiting to welcome him home. Mother had been gone ever since the ninth of March and Father now is coming from a long stay. "I have been so lonely and sad all these April days. They say he is dead, but I can't think he is. It is too much for me to believe. They have both gone away to stay and left us alone. We can't live without Papa."

The procession was now getting near. I would look with anxious eyes and heart to see Father, but could not see him. As the front wagon slowly moved up there, my eyes beheld a small black casket that contained the pale face and frail form of my father. All joy on earth and earth itself seemed to leave me. My heart within seemed to burst, but not a tear could I shed. I turned away to the kitchen. My coffee had turned to glowing coals of fire. I then left the house; never returned until called to join the procession that carried the remains of one I loved most dear to the cemetery and laid him away to rest by my mother to await the sound of the last trumpet, when they shall arise in glory to meet Christ with all the angels in the air and reign with Him forevermore, where there shall be no more parting pain nor death, where God shall wipe away all tears. He shall be our God and we shall be His people. What a glorious promise he has given us. Enough to console anyone old enough to consider His promises.

Chapter 6

Our Return Home
From the Burial

WE NOW RETURNED TO our home of desolation. The next I remember, Aunt Nancy Harkey came to where we were, above the house. Sitting upon some very large, flat rocks, not a word had I spoken. I was almost suffocating.

She was Mother's sister. She came with her heart overflowing with tears. "Children, oh, it is so hard. Come now, let's go to the house. I will have to go to my children. You must try to take care of what has been left you. Your pet sheep will be hard to keep out of the kitchen. They will soon destroy all your provisions. You have plenty left you to support you, if you will take care of it. If your Uncle William and me only lived near you that we could help you, I would be so much better satisfied, but we live so far it will be impossible for me to come often, but your Uncle William will come to see after you. Now, you must cheer up and keep a watch out for Indians. Don't let the little children get far from the house. Joe, you are the oldest. The greatest responsibility rests upon you. This is the fifteenth of April. The sixteenth of December you will be eighteen. Your father's request was for you to keep the children all together, but the little babe. Let your Aunt Caroline, your father's sister, keep him until he is old enough; then you are to bring him home too. It is a great responsibility on you, so young, but your father died perfectly

26

satisfied that you would manage his affairs just as well as he could. This is the most heartrending scene I've ever witnessed. Thirteen children inside of one month left orphaned; eight boys and five girls, the youngest not one month old, the oldest seventeen past." She coaxed us to the house and took their departure.

I had not yet shed a tear. It seemed that all was in a gloom and a hard pressure upon my breast. My two older brothers and my two older sisters were weeping bitterly at intervals, but the weight upon my breast remained solid and firm. Thus, days passed in gloom.

The boys carried on the general routine of business. The two older girls went ahead with the carding and spinning. We were left with a smokehouse full of bacon, wheat, corn, flour, and lots of feed, and a fine crop pitched. Uncle William advised my brother to sell all the bacon but just enough to run us through until fall, and lay in more supplies of dry goods and things we needed, which he did. We had 250 head of nice, gentle cattle and a nice bunch of stock horses, and plenty saddle horses, and work oxen; just a nice start to wealth. It was a very wet spring and the crop grew fast. Everything was looking fine.

The boys were plowing the corn; one running around it, the other breaking out the middle. My oldest sister went to our neighbors to get some instructions about some sewing. The next oldest girl was worming cabbage in the field on the north side of the creek. The boys were near the house on the south side, where they could see all going on at the house. Joe told me us little children might take pin hooks and catch a mess of perch. We were all busy throwing out perch when I thought I heard a terrible roaring west and said to the children, "Listen." We all dropped our hooks and ran out to see what it was. There were just eight of us. I soon saw it was a bunch of cow hunters, so I thought, coming rushing down from the head of the springs after a Negro riding a wild horse. I instantly ran up a large, spreading live oak tree, that inclined to stoop, to where its branches spread out some ten or twelve feet from the ground. I sat there watching the Negro. Finally, I glanced my eyes back over the followers and I never saw such a pretty sight. "It isn't cowhunters, Jim." As I glanced my eyes just above me forty or fifty steps, I saw an Indian standing. I spoke low to the children, "It is Indians." I thought they were all at the foot of the tree, but they had discovered it was

Indians and had gone to the house. The first one that got there ran in the house and shut the others out.

I sat perfectly still with my eyes set on the Indian just above me. He began moving toward me. As he came near, I noticed another just south of the tree about thirty steps while the first one was still approaching from the west, now within fifteen steps of the tree in which I was sitting. I kept my eyes on him, for I saw he was going to ride under the branches of the tree where I was sitting and he was sure to capture me. I never moved nor hardly breathed. When he got under the tree I was just above his head. He could have taken hold of me so easy, but he jerked out a pistol. I knew my doom was sealed when he passed a little from under me, which threw my back toward him. I closed my eyes tight to receive the shots between my shoulders. At that instant I could have stuck my finger in the bullet hole, it seemed so real. When I opened my eyes, I turned my head like an owl, not my body, to see what he was doing. He was standing just out from under the tree with the pistol still in his hand and his legs hanging and his feet covered with a pair of leather moccasins. He pranced the dun animal there awhile, then fired the pistol three times straight up in the air, then they both moved toward the house.

I now turned myself to watch and see what they aimed to do. There was eighty of them. They had strung out all around the field to surround the boys in the field, but they dropped the traces and mounted the horses and ran to the farm. The youngest got in the house first, grabbed the gun and got ready to fire when Joe, the oldest, hollered "Don't shoot." As he ran to get the gun, the Indians fired several times at him but, luckily, not a shot struck him. He fired several shots, when the Indians dropped over on the opposite side of their horses and swung for several minutes. I felt sure he had got them, when all at once, they threw themselves straight on their horses, gave a keen yell, and away they went around the field where they all collected together. My brother stood on the style block and would elevate his gun towards them every few minutes.

I now looked all around to see if I could see an Indian. Not seeing any, I left the tree and in a few seconds I was on the style block. I hadn't made any noise until then and I screamed manfully when I got there. Then Joe began to look to see how many was out. He found that Julie, my second sister, was out and he began calling for her, but received no answer. He had about decided they had captured her, when she came rushing in, but couldn't speak a word and wet to her knees. She had run and hidden among underbrush and then decided she wasn't safe, and so ran on, until her tongue had swollen out of her mouth. The next thought was, what had become of Jane, the oldest girl. She was at the neighbors, or had gone there, but Mr. Hall was not at home and the Indians had gone that direction. So, he mounted his horse and started to see about her and only went a short distance, when he met her coming home. She had seen the Indians and was hurrying home.

Now, Joe just had three cartridges left and the Indians seemed to be located all around us. Mr. Duncan lived five miles above us, so he thought perhaps he could get ammunition there, if they were not all massacred. The next day he got on a fine mare, the fastest we had, and taking advantage of the creek, he started for Duncan's. When he got near the Springs, he saw several Indians on the top of the hill south of the Springs. They were amusing themselves with a man's hat, throwing it up and, as it came down, they would cast their spear in it. He took roundence *[sic]* and went on. When he got there, they were all alive, but they were out of ammunition too. He learned there that the Indians had gone into a dry goods store fifteen miles above and taken every nice trinket that was pleasing to their eyes, and then set fire to the house. They also went into the Widow Lindley's house and took all nice skirts and ladies hats and dragged her feather beds out and ripped them open and scattered the feathers all over the place, then set fire to the house. They were all away from home. Now you can understand why I thought them so pretty. They wore the hats and shawls and skirts and nice trinkets, all strung about them in different ways until they were beautiful to behold, not knowing what they were, but ugly, cruel and horrible when I found them out.

My brother came home no better off for ammunition than he was when he left, but glad to know our neighbors were yet alive. There were only four families living on Richland Creek from the head to the mouth; that was Mr. Duncan's family, our family, or the Harkey children, Mr. Hall's family, three quarters of a mile below us, and Spencer Wood, five or six miles below.

Now, what was our next step for safety? Duncan and Hall thought best for the three families to all get together, so we all moved to Mr. Hall's then, next, to carry everything we could do without and hide it, for we expected to have our houses burned by the Indians. It was now the eleventh of May. The great rush of the Indians was on the ninth of May, about eleven o'clock in the morning, 1869.

Our millet was headed out and just as fine as I ever saw grow. It was the very best place to hide everything we could possibly do without. Father had so many nice, valuable books. We carried those books all out and hid them in the millet. It began raining and continued to rain for several days, which caused all a great loss. Most everything was damaged, more or less; some totally ruined. The Indians drifted down the creek and ran upon a bunch of cowhunters, eleven in number. They had a little skirmish with the Indians; one white man lanced by the Indians, several Indians wounded, but none killed on the battleground. The white men were not expecting Indians at that time of the moon. It broke up the cowhunt. All went home to see about their families; found all unharmed, with the exception of a severe scare. The Indians had divided up into squads, ransacking the whole county for horses. The white men kept out scouts, keeping a sharp watch out, but after they split up they dared not take any certain trail for fear some other squad would turn into the neighborhood and massacre the women and children. Not knowing what their number was, it seemed that the whole tribe was making a general raid through the country.

Chapter 7

Our Move to the Settlement

THE THREE FAMILIES WERE still together at Hall's residence, seeing after what they had with all caution and care. The neighborhood on the San Saba River knew we were yet alive and were awaiting an opportunity to safely guard us into their settlement as soon as safety would permit. Wagons and teams were brought and we were moved to the settlement on the San Saba River. All our stock was left, except our teams.

After the Indians made their raid and drifted west with all the horses they could get, and the scare of the people became cold, the boys went back and forth to cultivate the crop. This was so inconvenient and dangerous, too, they concluded to move us back home in the fall. So when time came to gather the corn, we moved back; not a neighbor nearer than the San Saba River. So often we would get severe scares, but our scalps were spared and I feel that we were protected by the all powerful God. We were now all together. Joe had brought the little babe home. He was now seven months old. Aunt Caroline only kept him one week after the death. She sent him to Aunt Nancy, Mother's sister. She nursed him from a bottle, which made it better for the girls to take care of him. Aunt Nancy had become so attached to him, she came to see about us more often than she otherwise would have come. Several times she took me home with her and kept me several weeks at a time. She always called me a "cake of tallow"; was very kind and motherly to me and I loved her dearly. I would get homesick sometimes before she could send me home, but I never worried about it. When she saw I wanted to go, she managed some way to send me.

There was a school in their neighborhood and Joe wanted to put me in school. Mr. Singleton lived two miles and a half from the school and Mrs. Singleton and baby were alone most of the time, and he proposed to my brother to furnish me a gentle pony to ride to school, if I would stay with his wife for company. It was a bargain at once. I entered the little twenty-five cent school, kept my pony staked at night, got up early, got our breakfast while Mr. Singleton milked and soon, off to school. I soon became very much attached to Mrs. Singleton and her to me. I had no trouble in making friends. While I never talked but very little, but always observing everyone's expression, then acting to please the expression. My desire was to be a friend to everybody, whereby I gained the friendship of everyone.

I always was very careful when I staked my pony, for fear she would get loose. Mrs. Singleton had a lady relative to see her; was to stay several days. She was raised on the frontier of Texas among the Indians. I had only been there six weeks, when I came from school that evening and staked my pony near the log hut where she could get all the nice mesquite grass she could eat. After supper, the two ladies were enjoying their conversation and having a nice time. I only sat and listened to their conversation and didn't take any part whatsoever. The dogs kept barking and rushing to the door and out again, as if they were tearing something to pieces. I felt uneasy about my pony, but she was staked within ten steps of the door. I hadn't heard her snort nor make any racket, but felt as if Indians might be near, but said nothing. Their conversation hushed. Mrs. Singleton's sister-in-law said, "Jany, I smell Indians. They are right here. I tell you they are. I have smelled them too often to be mistaken. It is a good thing we were talking loud as we were. They won't know but there is a dozen of us in here." We kept the old slab door well secured every night. All talk ceased. We were very quiet; sat and listened until very late. The dogs barked all night, but would go quite a distance from the house and not rush back. We knew by that they had left. Next morning, sure enough, they had cut my pony's rope and taken her off. There were moccasin tracks all around the house where, no doubt, they tried to get a view inside the house, but hearing so much noise they concluded there were too many to tackle.

Now I was left afoot; too far to walk to school. Aunt Nancy lived just across Wallace Creek from where I was staying. She thought likely I could get to stay with Mrs. McDaniels and go to school from there. As she only had one small girl and I could be so much help to her, and she was not strong either, Joe moved me to Mrs. McDaniels. I stayed there a short time. It was very rainy weather and the schoolhouse was on the opposite side of the river and, on account of high water, I never went to school anymore that term. I then went home.

The oldest boys had begun to incline to want to take up rough habits. All classes of boys were stopping in and lying around. No other stopping place on the road from the settlement twenty-five miles above the Colorado River to the settlement on the San Saba River, and our house was a regular hotel. The boys were very generous hearted, always caring for everyone and their teams and, as most all boys, loved company and they had never had the opportunity to have associates. They were being ensnared gradually, not observing it. They bought a violin first, then began playing cards for pastime. Next, they would go to the little rough dances, allowing their minds to drift from home duties. We all became more indifferent. We passed the time away in various ways.

I soon learned to play the violin well and delighted in the music. We would occasionally get severe frights by Indians, but it would soon get old to us and we would go on and not think anymore about them until another fright. Time passed on in a childish gloom to me, until the next summer my oldest sister married and she left us. She lived near a school. Joe put me with her to go to school again. I went awhile, but I formed such a dislike to my brother-in-law I became dissatisfied and brother took me home. My brothers were always so kind to me. I then stayed home. My married sister moved back near us and my next oldest sister stayed most of her time with my married sister and, as I was the third oldest girl, all the home duties fell on me when Julia was gone. Joe then let the fourth sister go stay with Jane, in order to get Julia back. Then one of my little brothers must stay with Jane while her husband was away.

There arose a discord between the four oldest children from some cause. They all three seemed to be against Joe. He never did get Martha and Jim back home. They made their home there bitterly against Joe's will. Julia would come home once every few days. I learned to keep house well and didn't care after taking the burden on my shoulders, though it was a trying one. My two oldest brothers were so good and kind to me, it caused the envy to increase in my sisters' hearts. I can't tell why they made the difference. I have shed tears about it. I could see they loved me so much better than Julia, and I thought she was so good, yet they didn't buy for her like they did for me. I've often thought that was why she didn't like to stay at home.

I remember well one great difference Joe made towards me. He went to San Saba and bought me a beautiful muslin dress and sent it out in my brother-in-law's wagon to his house for me. My sisters thought as Julia was older, she ought to have it. They didn't say anything to me about it. When he came home, he asked me how I liked my new dress. I told him I didn't have any new dress. "I bought you a new dress and sent it out to Jane's," was his reply. I went after it right then. I saw Julia wanted it so bad. Oh, I thought it a beauty. The next was how I should make it. I will put three ruffles on the skirt, all varying in width. That is very stylish now. I was now thirteen years old, could cut and make my own clothes to suit me. We had a neighbor now living in the old Brown residence, Mrs. Gurney. I never had made a ruffled skirt and needed some instruction. I went to her to know how to proceed about cutting the ruffles. I gained the desired information, went back, and went to work. It took me a whole week to finish up as I did the sewing with my fingers. I thought it the finest dress, but it still lacked something.

My second brother had come home; he had been working off. I showed him my new dress. "Oh John, if I just had some narrow blue ribbon to head each ruffle it would be so pretty."

"We will go to town and you can get it and I will pay for it," he said.

The next day we went to town. The first thing I saw was my narrow ribbon. Then I saw some blue and white plaid sash ribbon and my eyes seized it with desire. "John, wouldn't this be beautiful to wear with my dress?" "Get it if you want it; get what you want. I'll foot the bill."

Next was a real nice pair of shoes which I soon selected, then a nice hat. Now I could see myself in this new suit; then I thought of Julia and my proud heart faltered. "John, do you care if I get Julia some shoes and a sash?"

"No, get them if you choose," and then my spirit revived.

She was so proud of her presents and I felt much better to go home with a satisfied mind. I could not have felt happy in my new suit if I hadn't bought her something just as nice, too.

I now began to think there was some happiness in this world yet for me. I could play the violin well and was very attractive among the opposite sex. My brothers would have me go with them to the balls; I always helped furnish the music, which gave me a great delight. When I began playing, I soon gave attraction, and there would be crowds around me; although, I was never haughty and vain as some would have been.

Chapter 8

An Assault of a Reprobate

NOW THERE WAS TO BE a ball on the San Saba River and invitations were sent out to everybody and everyone attended, for there was no other kind of society to amuse people of the frontier and all classes were accepted in our social circle, but my inward instinct, from some unknown cause, always guided me to select the highest class of people for my near associates. So, my brothers made preparations for me to attend the ball. They had to go quite a little distance for their horses and there was a man boarding with our neighbor who had spent the night with my brothers, so when they were ready to go after the horses he was shaving and the boys said, "Mr. Crow, we will have to go after the horses. We won't be gone very long, not over an hour. You be contented and feel at home until we get back." I felt a presentiment of fear, but couldn't tell from what cause it possibly could come. I was sewing very busily and all my younger brothers and my little sister were having so much sport catching mice in the granary.

As soon as my older brothers left the house, a great fear came over me of the man they had left in the house with me. Although he had never spoken a word to me, he got up and started to sit down by me. I got up and went to the granary where my sister and brothers were and had them come in the house. I

36

told them I was afraid of the man and not to go out and leave me alone with him. They stayed awhile, satisfied, but in a little while their childish desire for sport of catching mice called them back to the granary. As soon as they were out, he made another start for me. I left the room and went to where the children were and told them I was going to slip off to my sister's, a mile above our house, and would go by the path under the bluff. "Don't you tell him where I am gone. I am so afraid of him." I started, going around the kitchen, so I thought he couldn't see me leave. I went a few yards when a thought presented itself to me, "He might follow me." I immediately turned and, sure enough, he was following. The first thought was to curse him. I can't tell why, but I began cursing and bemeaning him and he turned back. I ran in the house, got a shotgun, and marched him off. I stayed near the gun until the boys came, which was a couple of hours. He lost no time in leaving. They started in hot pursuit of him when they got in, but he took to the woods and they couldn't keep his trail. We never did hear of him anymore, nor did we ever think of the ball until it was over the next day.

I look back over my life and think of the frights I had. I wonder at me having any mind at all. We were always expecting Indians and often getting frightened when there were none near. We always looked to Joe for protection in everything. I loved him dearly, next to Father. He was so kind to me. I remember I had been to help my neighbor quilt and at noon I started home. It was in the fall of the year. I had pulled some grapes and was walking along with my head down, eating grapes, when all at once there came a rush of horses feet just in front of me. I glanced up; it was Indians. I was near the creek. I darted out of the road to the right and made for the creek and turned into it and ran a fourth of a mile, until I came to a deep hole of water with a high dirt bluff on the south. I lunged into the water up to my neck and stood perfectly still and listened until all sound of horses feet had faded away, then I left the water and started for home. When I got in hollering distance, I began calling, "Joe, Indians, Indians!" He came rushing to meet me affrighted *[sic]* to death. "Where are they, where are they?" he asked. Oh, I had such a rigor, I could hardly speak from the cold water and the fright. I told him they were going down the road. He sent me to the house and he went along the trail to see about how many there were in the bunch. He trailed on to our neighbors and found that it was him driving in a bunch of horses, instead of Indians, but the scare was none the less for me.

Now my second brother stayed away from home most all the time. They had both become careless in caring for the home affairs. Our farm had become a waste field for the cattle to browse in. No crops were raised at all, planting only for the stock to destroy and never taking heed to the repairing of fences, but still we had everything we needed. We were living off of what we had and nothing coming in, of which I never thought of. My great heart pressure had begun to soften. I could meditate over the loss of my parents and see the children scattering from home, which was against Father's will. I could now relieve my heartaches by the shedding of tears. I had begun to look into the future for more pleasant and happy days when, lo, my oldest brother began to stay away from home. He was compelled to leave us and work to support us. All those lonely days, we would pass off the time as best we could.

I now had a little brother who had learned to play the violin well. I would take my violin and sit on the doorstep and sing and play some sad piece until my streaming eyes could relieve my heart. Then I would give the violin to my brother and would get all the children on the floor and, to the music, I would teach them to dance. I would raise my frock that they could see my feet so they could learn the steps.

Thus, I passed my gloomy spells away. Sometimes we would go fishing, but I was of a restless disposition and, when quiet, I was very despondent and gloomy. My second sister had married now and I only had one sister with me, the youngest, little Annie; the prettiest and sweetest thing on earth, I thought. When the boys would come home, they were warmly welcomed. We would have our shooting matches. We would blaze a tree and then see who could make the best shots, which was fine sport for me. Then we would run foot races and jump flatfooted with weights and without weights, then half-hammered. I always took part in their amusement, whatever it was.

As time passed, all our sustenance went with it. We finally came to want. Joe had been off and when he came home, we told him we hadn't a dust of flour or meal. Flour was $15 per barrel and he had no money. I never will forget how he looked. He turned so pale and kept walking the floor, walking to the barrel and looking back and forth. Oh, I was so sorry for him. "I haven't a cent of money," he said. "Is there anything to eat?"

"No, not a mouthful of anything. We haven't had anything to eat for two days. We had broiled all the meat rinds and had eaten them two days before you came."

"I must hunt work," he said. The burden was now upon him alone. "I can't see you all hungry. I will go get a job splitting rails. That is all the kind of work there is to do." He went and got a contract to split several thousand. He got flour from the men to work on and lived on bread and water until he drew some money on his work.

I sent the little children to my sister's, but I thought I would stay and starve before I would go to my brother-in-law for anything to eat. My sister stayed with me. I had resolved in my mind to stay at home and could bear my hunger until relieved by death.

We hunted for eggs on the third morning. Oh, we were very hungry. We only found one and we roasted it and divided it, which only increased our hunger. Sister said, "Let us go to Jane's. We will starve and there is no use in starving." I finally gave over to go, but we only stayed a day and a night until Joe brought some flour home and came after us and had us go home. He got some milk cows up. Now, he had provided milk and bread for us. He said, "Now, stay at home and I will go back to work and will bring you more bread when I draw more money on my work, which will be before you run out again. Now, be as saving as possible." Then he took his departure and went back to splitting rails all alone in the woods, earning bread by the sweat of his brow for eight little orphans, which was a task at his age, and no encouragement, only my own kindness to him.

My whole soul went out in sympathy for him and I longed to see his return, which was before we had consumed our bread he had left us. If he had neglected and squandered to our want, he still had a manly heart and a soul of sympathy for us that no one else had, which found my love toward him almost like a father. He was all the one I had left now to look to. I would watch and wait his return home with all anxiety of a child toward a father. He continued to labor for our bread with all honesty and uprightness of a man, but found it difficult to keep bread for so many children, to say nothing of raiment for our bodies.

As a matter of coincidence, our garments would all soon be threadworn. I could see all this in the future and would look on my little sister and brothers with a sad, heavy heart. I sat and cried for the poor little things often and over again and wondered, "How are we to get clothes?" I would think of every worn out garment and how much could I get out of those old garments. "I will gather them up and see. Yes, I can get little waists out of the best part of those shirts." I would rip them up and make garments for the little brothers and would patch their pants when it would seem impossible to mend them, but when I succeeded to get them clothes, my heart gained relief.

Thus, I continued all summer long and until autumn began to show forth her brown leaves, when I was seized with chills and fever. Brother would provide medicine for me and get them stopped, but the malaria was still in my system, which kept me very melancholy and sad. He was compelled to leave home and earn bread, which caused our desolate home to be filled with solitude. So dreary! Oftentimes I would be seized with chills before he would get home. My little brothers would minister all help that was possible, which could not be very much excepting the preparation of the commonest kinds of hot tea of which I would give instruction to cool my terrible thirst and reduce my fever. The dear little things were so kind and obedient. I never have yet seen children that were their equals. I loved them with all my soul and they were kind to me and always looked to me as a mother for everything, and I felt a great responsibility hanging over me in regard to the rearing of them to manhood and womanhood. While I, myself, was only a child, I was constantly watching over them, keeping all dishonest thoughts and any evil actions from them whatever, except our pastime of home amusement of dancing of which I have never regretted yet. I feel that it was a pastime of great importance to increase our home ties so perfectly that we were able to bear our hardships and trials, and hold us together according to the prayers of our parents.

Chapter 9

My Duty at Home With Two Little Nieces and Youngest Brother

MY HEALTH BECAME POOR and I came down with chills and fever, and it seemed as though we couldn't break up the chills permanently, and Joe wanted to gather pecans. He told me if I took the chills to go to Mr. Singleton's, who now lived near us, and stay until he got back. In a few days my married sisters and their husbands pitched a pecan gathering also. My oldest sister's two little daughters, aged three and one- and one-half years old, were too small to be of any service in gathering pecans, so they sent them to me to care for while they gathered pecans.

In a couple of days I was seized with another rigor; there alone with nobody to minister to my needs. As soon as my fever subsided enough that I could walk, I took the three children, with my head reeling and bursting with pain, and made my way to Mr. Singleton's. They were very kind to me. We stayed there four days when the little girls, like all other children, began to have discord over their dolls. My disposition was never to be burdensome to anyone and, as I was, I couldn't assist Mrs. Singleton in the least. It worried me so I concluded, on the fourth day when my fever went down, I would take the children and go to my sister's residence, which was only a few hundred yards from Singleton's. So, when I felt that I could make it, I told Mrs. Singleton the little girls got along so bad it kept me nervous, so I would

41

take them to Jane's. She insisted that I should stay with her, but I
felt it would be best to go. It was now afternoon and the chills
came on in the morning, so I took the children and went. I managed to prepare supper and breakfast for them. As for myself, I
had no appetite whatever. My chills came as usual the next morning. Oh, such a fever as I had! I scarcely knew anything all day.
The children wandered about the place until evening, when Julia
and her husband came in and found me lying with a burning
fever and such a terrible pain in my side, I could hardly breathe.

Now, our old neighbor had returned to their old home lately
and Mamma Brown, as everyone called her, was called for. She
was kind to everybody and a good nurse too, and always treated
her own family in common sicknesses. She applied mustard plas-
ters to the pain and gave spirits of nitre to reduce the fever. She
stayed with me all night, and the next morning I was nearly clear
of fever, but my chill came earlier and every one worse until my
brother came the fourth day. He and Mamma Brown did everything they knew to ward off the chill, but failed. He then called in
a Botanic Doctor. He gave instructions of what herbs to get and
how to prepare the medicine and how to give it, and told them to
be punctual; not to allow another chill to come on, for it was
congestion and the next would take me off. They followed direc-
tions strictly and kept it off, but the pain left my side so afflicted
I couldn't straighten for two weeks. I had no appetite for anything and I was kept under the influence of medicine until everything had a sickening smell.

My brother-in-law had slaughtered a beef and he was very
fond of broiled beef kidney. He brought it in on a stick and began broiling it, and I got the scent of it and it smelled good. I
spoke about it and he brought it to the bed, with a piece of bread,
and cut and fed me several bites. I thought it was the best meal I
was ever served in my life. I began to slowly improve and in two
weeks I was able to go home.

I can see that home of desolation now, and see the half-
clothed and half-fed little brothers and little sister. They had
stayed there and done the best they could toward caring for each
other and managed to cook their bread and milk; the milk they
drank while Joe would be away. I was not able to do anything but
could give Levi, the oldest little brother, instructions how to man-

age our scant affairs. He would go out and kill a squirrel and stew it for me to eat and make me tea; just as kind as he could be.

I was so pale and thin and just at an age to have a mother's advice in regard to my feminine sex so that I could know how to care for my health as I should, but no one gave me any advice, whatever, in regard to the nature of the feminine sex. I was merely a child, yet I was womanly in my ways and even had a lover who was gone west at that time, but when he returned he proved false to me, which was a severe wound to my heart, added to my afflictions. I dwindled all through the winter, a perfect skeleton. I could not give him up, it seemed, but when spring came it gave me better hopes. My health improved and a fresh color came to my cheeks for the first time in my life, yet I was not in perfect health by any means.

Joe continued to work, coming in every week. In April he learned that there had been money appropriated for a three month school in our neighborhood, which delighted him as well as myself. He provided us the necessary books and started us all to school except the three youngest, which were under the scholastic age. I would take them to school with me. They were no trouble at all, though it was very tiresome to the little fellows. I would cook our bread without soda or seasoning, except salt, fill bottles with fresh milk, and get off to school on time every morning. At noon I would get the children and get off to one side to eat our tough bread and sweet milk, for I well know how people looked on us as an object of pity; yet, never providing those things needful to the body. I was very sensitive and kept a close watch over the little ones. I could not bear to see them stured *[sic]* in the least, if they were half-clothed and fed. I thank God He gave us a perfect heart and rational minds and talents to make friends. Even if our home was destined to poverty, everyone was my friend. We all learned fast and I soon was ready for the fourth reader, and it was wonderful how I began to master mathematics, but the school was soon out and we had only got nicely started.

Now Joe, finding it difficult to feed and clothe us by his day labor, enlisted as a Texas Ranger to be away from home all the time. We were about destitute of everything when he left. Oh, how it grieved me to see him saddle Old Charly, our family horse, and take the last blanket our dear mother's hands had woven and leave us alone; going out to be scalped by the Indians in the first skirmish, but he said, "This is the only chance to provide for you children. I will send you money on the first payday," which would be sometime in the winter. He departed and I turned away with a heavy heart and went to the house. Taking up my violin and sitting down upon the doorstep, I played and wept all alone, for the children were out at play. I couldn't see how we were going to get along.

Soon the hot summer days came. Mother's old spinning wheel was still here. "I will get it out and there are cards and there is wool the children have sheared from those dead sheep. I can spin thread and knit socks for sale. I can get fifty cents per pair." I went to work. I would spin my thread and knit socks and sell and buy such as we had to have, but couldn't begin to supply our need. Winter was coming and all were in need of clothes. I was barefooted. "What am I to do? I will see Charley Willson and see if he will buy three pairs of socks. That will get me a pair of shoes." I went to see if he would buy them and he said he would. I had only one pair done and I gave them to him and went to knitting. He went to town the next day and bought the shoes, but never would take the two pair of socks due him. I often think of him yet. There was a kindness in my heart toward him, although he is now sleeping under the sod awaiting the Judgment Day.

I could realize our great necessities for winter and it was near at our door. Here we were without the necessary cover to keep us warm through the cold, bleak nights of winter. There were some pecans near us on the creek, but not one on our land. There was nothing thought of gathering pecans off of anyone's land in those days, so I took the children and began gathering. Levi was my climber, twelve years old he was, and we gathered and tugged them in the best we could without a horse even; just on our shoulders. We gathered several bushels.

Now, I well knew the peddler would never come to our home, for we hadn't anything to sell, so I kept a watch for him to make his appearance at Brown's. In the course of a week, I saw him drive up. Soon, the next morning, I set out to Brown's. He had calico and dry goods of different kinds. I first got his price on pecans, then the prices of his goods, then I made a calculation in my head about how much I would be able to buy. I first got material to make the children clothes, then a dress for myself, and the balance in goods to make comforts for covering.

You can't imagine how proud I was. I went to work and made up the clothing first, then went to quilting. I soon had cover for our beds, but our house had begun to let in the sunshine and rain. The little boys would bring up driftwood for firewood and, if it didn't rain or snow, we kept warm enough, but if it rained or snowed, we could do nothing better than to lie still. If it only rained and then cleared up, we could dry everything the next day, but when we had a long, wet spell it was so disagreeable. Oftentimes it would be night after night I was compelled to go to bed and everything wet. Sometimes we would carry the bed clothes to the fire and warm them before we would lie down on them. I can't see how we lived. To think over it now, it doesn't seem that I could have borne it but, with the help of our dear Master, we were carried over the great turbid sea.

All during this time I received letters from Brother. I was always glad to get his letters, but I never read a letter from him without shedding tears. About the 15th of December I received a letter from him. When I opened it, I found enclosed a $50 bill. Now, you can imagine how I felt, but I took a long cry, then began to think, "Here are the children all barefooted and the roof lets in the sunshine and rain." I couldn't decide what was best to do.

Mr. Hall came one day and I thought I would get his idea of what it would cost me to have the repairing done. "It will cost you at least $40," he said, "perhaps more." I knew then I would have to give up the idea of repairing, for the children must have shoes and warmer clothes.

Joe wrote me to go to San Saba and buy such things as we needed, so I concluded I would make arrangements to get to town. I made the arrangement, but I hadn't a decent dress to wear. I went to Manerva Brown and asked her if she would be so kind as to loan me a dress to wear to town. She granted me the favor and Levi and myself put out. We got shoes for all, then jeans for the little boys' pants, and coats, and got my little sister several dresses and myself a worsted dress and a calico dress, and material for other purposes and had $30 left. Now I felt independent. I had money to buy food too. We came home happy.

I went to work making up the clothes, which was a task to make so many suits, saying nothing of my own and sisters, but I lost no time. Christmas was near at hand and I wanted my new dress by Christmas. I worked late and early and by Christmas I had my nice dress completed. It was real nice and now I could attend the dances, of which I took a great delight. My second brother came home to take Christmas, which made everything so much pleasanter for me. The young people visited us often during the holidays. We were now all very presentable; could give our friends comfort, at least, and I attracted not a few with my violin. I had many suitors but none I thought very ideal, but don't understand me to be a flirt; I was far from it. I never attended dances unless one of my brothers could be with me. I felt it so much out of place for me. If one of them couldn't accompany me, I stayed at home.

This was a happy Christmas for me. It was nice, pretty weather all through the holidays. The two Brown girls, Manerva and Rebecca, lived near us. They often stayed with me when I would be so lonely. I loved them like sisters. Our neighborhood consisted of several neighbors now; enough to have a singing school. We all would meet every Sunday, carry our dinners, spend the whole day and have a nice time on Sunday, and through the week have our dances. Every time brother's Company came near home, he came in to see how we were getting along; never stayed very long when he came. He always helped me cook while there.

The first time he came, after sending me money, was the summer following. I got all the money that was left and gave it to him, as I felt he ought to have it, but he handed it back to me and said, "Keep it to buy what you need. I will try to send you more before that is gone." I felt so grateful to him.

When he would come in, we would all gather around him to hear of his exploits and hear him tell of the skirmishes he had been in, and how he would run his knife around the Indian's scalp and pop his foot on his neck while he yet groaned, grab the top of the scalp and pop it off while alive. His scout was just from Trimble County, where they ran onto a squad of nine Indians. There were only seven Rangers. He said it was the greatest fun; just like a bunch of wild hogs. When they came up on an Indian, they would shoot him down, jump off their horses, grab him by the hair of the head, pop their foot on his neck, cut around the scalp and give it a jerk and it would crack like a whip; the Indian still groaning. I could hardly bear it. I said, "Oh, Joe, how could you be so cruel; poor things?"

"Ah," he said, "We had no time to meditate. We were gone

after another right then, until we scalped seven and captured nine of their horses and wounded the other two, but they got away to tell the tale on one horse. We routed every crook and creek, but we never found them. It was fine sport. They never did attempt to fight at all; just went helter-skelter from the bounce; made it fun to us boys. We had no fight at all. We boys sure got the big end of that squad." They sent the scalps and ponies to headquarters and struck out east, in by home, and stopped twenty-four hours with us. This was in May or June of 1873.

John was in and out. He worked with cowboys and had no care of the present or future; a whole-souled fellow. He had lots of friends and lots of scraps, but never amounting to anything. He always spoke just what he thought; let it hit or miss. I never felt that he was responsible to us for a living. He seemed like one of the children, and Joe my father. John was kind to me and would help me work or do anything for me he could. He was always ready to take me to a dance. He was all sport. No responsibility rested on him. When he had any change, I knew I would get it, but he seldom had much nor did he want much. Though he was my brother and I loved him, Joe and him didn't agree, and that grieved me no little. They never stayed at home together long at a time, but all the little brothers were kind to each other and I seldom ever had to scold them.

One day I told Annie and Dee to go bring a fresh bucket of water. I put the stick under the pail, gave Dee one end and Annie the other end, and they started. They got off a piece and began fussing. I told them to go on and behave, but they kept fussing. I told them to bring me a switch and come back. They went and hunted the thorniest mesquite limb they could find and slipped up to me, so full of laughter, and handed it to me. It amused me so, I could hardly speak for laughing, but I put on a stern face and looked them straight in the eyes. "Do you want me to strike you with this thorny stick?" They stood a moment and burst out in a laugh. I could hardly keep back the laugh, but I did. I told them to go on now after the water. You can't imagine how I laughed when they were gone.

I always thought my brothers so cute and smart, and Annie a perfect little angel. Mose, younger than Dee and next to the baby, was a monkey and a dancer; always made the boys give him a nickel before he would dance. They would tell him to dance ten minutes and they would give him a nickel. He never refused when the money came in sight. Eli, the baby, was a sad little thing and never seemed to have any pleasant thoughts. It grieved me because he looked so sad. No one ever had anything to say to him like they did to Mose.

The little fellows caused me great anxiety and uneasiness during the summer. They would slip off to the creek and roll in rocks for pastime. One day two men from the Colorado River stopped for dinner. While I was cooking dinner, the boys slipped off to the bluff and engaged in their sport. Just as we sat down, I heard one of the children coming, crying. My first thought was that the other two were drowned. I left the table at a dash, John after me. We soon met Dee and asked him what was the matter. He told us Mose and Eli were drowned. When we got there, Mose was out and showed us where they fell in. Eli had on a red slip. John plunged in and saw the dress under water. He had sunk the last time. He brought him up to the bank and I seized him in a frantic. He was dead in my arms, and I started off in a run. Mr. Singleton caught me, took him from me and took hold of his heels, turned his head down, shook the water from his stomach and rolled him over and over, rubbing him too. After so long he said, "He is reviving. He is not dead." When his pulse was good, he took him to the house and rolled him on a barrel until circulation was good, then wrapped him up. He then questioned Mose to how he got out. He said, "I catched to two little woots and pulled out." One was two years old past, the other three years old past, Dee five years past; all too young to know what danger was. The baby was able to walk by night again, but was stupid several days.

So the summer passed with so many mishaps. My little sister and little brothers, that fall, were playing with corn stocks and she made a leap on the corn stock. It broke and gave her such a jar. I carried her in dead, so I thought, but after working some time, we brought life back.

I was a natural, sympathetic nurse with the children and our dog, Ballie. We all loved him. Levi and Jeff made him kill every skunk they struck and he went deranged. We tied him after he had been shot in the tail and had worms in him. We concluded we would cut his tail off and sear it with a hot iron. Levi and Jeff held him. One of the children held his tail on the log, and I chopped it off, then slapped the red hot iron to him and seared the wound. We then turned him loose. He went and took his tail and buried it. Oh, we were so horrified at what he had done, we all felt like crying. As winter was nearing he recovered, to our joy, for he was our guard.

Now our thoughts began to reach out to winter again, in dread to know how we could ever get through another winter safe, but among all the dreads there was some happiness. John wanted me to go to a dance on the San Saba River. It was a nice, warm morning. I washed that morning and my clothes froze before they dried. About three o'clock in the eve we started and, of course, I was not clothed sufficiently for such a spell. When we got to the San Saba River, it was up half-side deep. He took me across first and helped me off to go back after his girl, and when I struck the ground I couldn't stand; my foot was frozen. He brought her across on my horse, put me up on my horse, and we went on. I think that was the coldest night I ever felt in my life. I never suffered as much in my life with cold.

We left the next evening. Jasper Brown gave Becca and me whiskey and took us two miles to an aunt's. When our horses got out of the water, their tails were a shield of ice. When we got to the fire and began to get warm, I couldn't see or stand. I fell over on a turnout bed, but no one knew it. I was not well all through the winter. Such melancholy spells I had all winter.

Chapter 10

Another Three Month School

THUS, I PASSED THE dreaded winter and when spring came, it brought with it a promising future for me. I had become less melancholy. The boys were away from home, it was true, but we were better provided for and Joe would send us money and we could get along. Our fear of the Indians was now thought but little about, and we were fairly well clothed.

Now we were to have another school, which delighted me more than anything else, with the same teacher, Mr. Riley; a fine teacher too. When school began, I took the children and started in the first day. The teacher took a great interest in me. I was quick to learn anything he put me at, although very much behind all the girls of my age. They had had some opportunity and were carrying several studies I had never taken up; mental arithmetic and grammar. He told me to get me a grammar and a mental arithmetic book, so I did so. He started me alone. All the large girls and boys were so far ahead of me, but I set out to overtake them. In a short time I caught them. I discovered their envy toward me, but I never seemed to notice it. We went along together for awhile.

The teacher saw I was held back, so there was one of our neighbor boys in our class who was twenty-two years old, Nute Brown. He was as good as myself. We had been raised together.

We had lived as neighbors ever since I was home, with the exception of six or seven years when they lived in Bell County. Now we both certainly did work. I tried to leave him and he tried to leave me, but we finally gave it up, so we went along together, perfectly satisfied to take each other as classmates. We certainly enjoyed our studies.

I will never forget Mr. Riley teaching me how to step land. He had me get up on the floor and step paces. The girls looked at me with horror, but he said, "Never mind what anyone says. You may marry a man who can't do this and if you do, you can be of great help to him." (And so I did.) I have stepped and measured land often times for my husband and do all his calculating. So I just let them look in wonder. I never hesitated one second for any frown they made. I never lost a day.

I would do my washing on Saturdays with the help of my little brothers, and all mending and household affairs. I always had to go to the creek to wash, which made a great task. Nute would come to where we were washing and we would work problems all day. We became great associates. I finally took rheumatism in one of my lower limbs. Oh, it was painful on arising of mornings! I could scarcely walk, but I was so determined to go to school, I would start hopping along. By the time I got to the school, the walk caused free circulation of the blood and I would be free from pain until I would get quiet then, my, how I would suffer! I would try not to limp so the young men would not discern my feebleness, but it would show on me in spite of my grit. The teacher would have me go to the board. When I would arise, it would almost make me holler. He would say, "What's the matter with your foot, Sarah?" I would answer, "Nothing," and drag along to my work. When excused, I could hardly get to my seat. I suffered all through the school in this way.

Now, Joe was a natural mathematician. No one could turn him down on the most difficult problem if given a slate and pencil, but to take a difficult problem and solve it mentally was hard for him. So, when he would come home, he would visit our school. I saw he was delighted with my progress in school, which gave me encouragement. When our mental class was called, he took his seat with us to recite with us, but he couldn't master the problems in his head, so Mr. Riley says, "Sarah, help him out," which I did. It certainly encouraged me, for I well knew he was good in mathematics. He had solved problems for teachers previously, and was known everywhere that he was almost perfect in figures, but he had never made use of the mental method. When recess came, he said, "Now, Sis, when you want any books, send and get them. You are progressing so nicely in your studies." After bidding us farewell, he took his departure. It grieved me to see him leave, but was rejoiced in the promise of new books, for I was then in need of a fifth reader. I sent after my reader the first chance I got. It seemed as valuable to me as gold. When I received it, I soon took the contents of it. Then my interest was grammar and mathematics, but the term was so short I never accomplished as much as I wished to.

School was out the last of May, but there was hardly a week elapsed, and often not a day, but what Nute came and we would get down to our problems. What one couldn't master, the other could. Time passed in this way for two months when Nute concluded he would make a successful peddler. So he started out as a peddler. I again became so lonely. He seemed so near to me; always giving me advice, just like my brother. I saw him no more, only to bid him good morning and pass a short conversation of livelihood and friendship, and bid him farewell again.

In disgust, I was seized with chills and fever again. I would have a chill every other day regular. My brothers were both away from home. My little brothers would gather cottonwood bark and boil it down and make a strong tea for me to take as a substitute for quinine. Oh, such a dose it was, but was all right to take it for chills, and castor oil, cayenne pepper, and turpentine as a laxative; half of a teacup full at a dose. I would get the chills stopped, but the seventh day I would have another one.

I finally concluded I would try exercise to ward them off. When my chill day came, I waited until I felt the symptoms and I jumped up and began dancing. I kept it up until my fever began to bulge very high and finally gave it up and went to bed. Oh, my, I certainly paid for my dancing.

In a few days one of the little boys took a chill, a little later another, and finally everyone of us was down with chills and fever. Some days everyone was down at the same time. Oh, I felt like we were parentless, friendless, and poor. Everybody was too busy to minister to our needs, but there is a time coming when everyone of those people will have to answer to this accusation.

Paul says pure and undefiled religion before God is to visit the orphaned and widowed in their afflictions, and keep yourself unspotted before the world. It grieved me greatly. I would just lie and think, "If I ever do see anyone lying helpless like we are, I would certainly minister to their needs." I would lie there and think over our condition until I could no longer bear it, just to see them all lying so sick and no one to hand them water. I would arise with my head bursting with pain, prepare hot mustard water, and begin sponging the one that was the sickest, and so continued until I sponged all in this way. I cooled their fever with the help of sage tea, drunk hot.

I never will forget a widow lady passing by one day and, stopping in, found us all down and the beds filled. She went to everyone and examined our fever and said, "Oh, my, this is awful. Why, I don't see what you are all to do." I knew what we were to do; that was, to be patient and do the best we could, but just her presence there a little while gave me some comfort. She showed her sympathy towards us and if she could have helped us, I felt as though she would, but she was a very poor lady with three little children to support and I knew she had a hard time herself. There were others near us that could have helped us, that showed no help.

Thus we were, until Brother's Company came near and he came home to see after us. He lost no time in getting chill tonic to break it up, which was not but a few days after we began the tonics. He went off again and left us. My second brother was out west working on a ranch, but he didn't feel the interest in us that Joe did. He was younger and really not of the disposition Joe was. Joe was our stay and our only helper in time of need and deserves a royal crown in the last day. There shall always remain a great vacancy in my heart for him. No matter what he might do, no matter how low he might degrade himself, if I could lift him up, it would give my heart joy to do so.

Now, autumn was near ready to make us her yearly visit again. I began preparation for her. I would piece quilts with my scraps, of which I had several ready to quilt. I went to work and quilted all those quilts. Next, I bought cloth and made up the children's clothes, then spun thread and knit their socks and my little sister's stockings, which occupied my entire time up to the very last month of autumn. When completed, I felt free and

could pass off my time with my violin. After supper was over, I
would take it and play for the children to dance. Oftentimes they
could hear my music at Brown's. He always kept work hands and
he had two beautiful daughters, Manerva and Rebecca. Often the
girls and the young men would surprise me with their company,
then I would give them music awhile and then turn the violin
over to my little brother; whereupon, we would all join in a dance
to his music and have a real nice time.

I had, by now, entirely given up my old lover; never thought
of him as a lover anymore. There was a young man in our community that I knew would love to pay his respects towards me,
but I never encouraged him in the least. One night he came with
them. It seemed that I admired him all during our social conversation, more than anyone else. I could realize my condition of
poverty and very well knew all the regards the young man had for
me could not be other than for my personal modesty and ladylike
manner. I conducted myself as a lady and was regarded as a lady
by everyone, old and young. The old ladies visited me, as well as
the young ladies. I could entertain all ages, even little children.
When they visited my brothers and little sister, I would take an
active part in their amusement too, which caused all to love my
company. I was a great mimic of any action or speech, with which
I amused the girls often. After my heart lightened, I was very
jolly; always playing tricks on some of the girls. It amused me.

I went to visit Rebecca one day and she had gone to her
sister's. We were great chums and I awaited her return. I thought
it would be sport to play a trick on her. I told Manerva what I was
going to do. I went in the room and gathered up the raggedest
suit I could find, blacked up, put on an old flopped hat and
watched for her appearance. The house was situated on the
north side of the creek. I would come from the south side after
she came down the south bank. She would turn up the channel
several steps, then up a steep hill. Just at the yard fence there was
a deep hollow, just east of the crossing on the north side. I con-
cealed myself there and when she came down the south bank and
started west, I put in after her, just as she went to go up the bank
on the north side. I was within ten feet of her, making a dreadful
noise to attract her attention. She had large brown eyes and when
she turned and saw me, her eyes projected out so much, I could
have knocked them off with a stick, it seemed to me. She wheeled

and gave a holler, "Lord, God, a little nigger, a little nigger," climbing the hill at the same time. Just as she got to the fence, I caught her. I roared with laughter, but she couldn't laugh, after knowing it was me. I had scared her nearly out of her wits. I said in my heart, "I am not ever scaring anyone else," and I kept it.

Now, our community was in need of a minister of the Gospel, so Parson King was called to preach once a month for us. I always attended and took a great interest. I always wanted to be a Christian, but I couldn't understand his teaching as I did Father when I was a small child. He didn't expound the Gospel to suit the desire of my soul, but still I felt that I would get religion after awhile. I continued to be on time every month.

Winter came on and my second brother came home. Now they must have a dance. Christmas would soon be here and I must get in practice for Christmas. So we had a dance. We all went. I always had an escort, but John would be in our company too, or somewhere near, but the one I admired almost never indulged in dancing. He would go, but never take any part, except to talk with the young ladies. He would always sit near me when I was playing the violin. I saw I had him captivated, but went along, had a nice time with all the young men alike. We had a wonderful, good time all through Christmas. After Christmas, our dances stopped and I went down to see a cousin of mine at the mouth of the creek. When I started home, the young man I admired was in that neighborhood. As natural as can be, he was going home too, so he escorted me home and it suited well to my part, I will say.

Now I turned my interest to church service again. His parents were church members, but not Methodist. He was my constant escort to all gatherings and gave me regular calls.

Now spring began to peep forth. Soon all nature shown forth all her beauties; so glorious to my young heart; more beautiful to my soul than I ever could have dreamed it possible to be. Everything shown some nature of happiness to me. My heart was light and gay. Now our protracted meeting was coming on. I made preparations for us all to attend regular. The little boys needed another pair of pants and I had some white duck. I gathered Shoneyhaw *[sic]* bushes and colored it a navy blue and pressed the goods and cut and made them a pair of pants. While I was pressing the pants, my teacher called on me. "Oh, that is a beautiful color," he said. "What kind of goods is it, Sarah?"

"This is duck."

"Why, I never saw that color of duck."

I then told him it was my coloring. He seemed so astonished and complimented me very highly. I thanked him, courteously, for his compliment and kept busy at my work, for I had no time to lose. The meeting would begin the next night.

We attended regularly. It was a Revival meeting. I tried to get religion, but never could have that miraculous change. I went up as a mourner all the first week. I tried to get my constant escort to go up and be prayed for, but he didn't think religion could be found at the mourner's bench, but I thought I would surely have a change if only I could continue to be prayed for. Some would get happy and go off in trances, but I never felt the least change.

On the second Sunday, Rebecca and myself were knelt down close together and a dog crawled under the bench we were kneeling on and smelled bad. We thought we would drive him away and not make any disturbance. We finally got tickled and we never did get over it until the preacher dismissed us. Oh, I was mortified at my conduct. I said then, I would never go to a mourner's bench again. I felt I had committed a great sin, but I could not help it. I made my word good and the meeting closed at the end of two weeks and I was none the better in religious respect, but my lover and me had come to a thorough understanding during the meeting.

Now, the community had built a new schoolhouse on the eastern portion of Brown's land. It was known as the Brown's Schoolhouse. They couldn't get Mr. Riley to teach this year, so they employed Mr. McNeal. I was anxious for school and started the first day. He was a very good teacher, but he didn't instruct as well as Riley, according to my opinion. He had us take up too much time making preparations to entertain our visitors on Fridays. This I enjoyed, and took a great interest in. Nothing pleased me better than to act my part in dialogues. I became McNeal's favorite in school, too. This, of course, wasn't pleasant to my schoolmates, but I was always kind to them all. They couldn't help being my friends. I wouldn't allow them to be otherwise.

I didn't accomplish much this school term. I gained some knowledge of elocution and permanently established what I had learned previously. He never taught mathematics mentally, and it seemed a slow method to me to take time to work a problem on my slate, but I was very pleased. I was more advanced than I thought of being. Now, the scholastic age was from eight to eighteen. I only had one more year after this school term. I knew Joe could never pay my tuition. It grieved me to think of it, but I thought, "I'll get all out of this I can."

Now, my lover would visit our school often. He came to visit us one Friday evening and, as we walked home, he told me he had hired out to drive a bunch of beef cattle to Kansas. I had previously noticed little faults in him, and when one begins to look on anyone for faults, they are sure to find them. We are then looking through blue glasses. If we were free from faults, we would never look for faults of others. June love hides a multitude of sin. After he told me of his intended journey, he asked me to write to him. He couldn't write himself, but would get a friend to write me where to address my letter. I promised I would, but I was holding a jealous heart toward him, already, because of a prosperous young lady in the community. I felt he treated me somewhat wrong in favor of this girl, but never mentioned it to him. He was to start on Monday morning, and said he would come by the schoolhouse and tell all farewell. I kept my eyes open, to be sure if I was right, before he took off. I was certain in my mind he loved another. If he could get her, he would cast all love on her. I received his address, Ellsworth, Kansas, but that was all. When he came home, he came to see me.

"Why was it you failed to write me at Ellsworth, Kansas?"

"Really, because I knew you would love another for her wealth, if you thought your love wouldn't be cast away, and leave me in poverty," I said. He was grieved at my speech, but it never lessened my opinion in the least, yet I tried not to think so.

I was almost in love with another, I must say. I wanted time to see if I really did love someone else. Our school was now closed and I was now at home most all of the time. My lover still made his regular calls and I very well knew my love was not true. I was always pleased when another called on me. When spring opened again, it brought another change in me which caused my mind to worry. I would think over the past and wonder, "What am I? I have always tried to be honest and true to my word. Am I deceived in myself? Surely I am. This is not my nature." Oh, how I wished I could regain a few months back. "I have experienced the pangs of grief caused by a false lover. I will never bring such grief to anyone. I will see if there isn't a way out of this and not purge my conscience. Time will bring all things right and, from an honest heart, it shall be peace instead of agony."

There was a schoolmate of mine that lived on the Colorado River, a beautiful blonde she was, and very well known. "She enjoys my lover's company and school will soon begin again and I will manage to get her between us. He likes her company and is liable to fall in love with her, if he has any doubts of me, and she is nice and pretty, too. I think she is sure to fall in love with him. Her father is a prosperous farmer and owns considerable stock, too; just the girl for him." So, school began and we all started to school. Josephine came over and entered school. When he came to visit our school on Fridays at recess, Josephine and myself were together all the time. When he approached me in conversation, I would cause her to become engaged in our conversation, too. Thus it went for several weeks and, at last, I saw it would work all right. I never had encouraged anyone else yet. He finally escorted her to singing and that gave a loop for me, yet I made no complaint. He still liked the girl's company that lived in our community, but I knew she was engaged to another man. He couldn't come in there.

I finally began to be distant and indifferent towards him; then he would respect her the more. I just wrote him a note, telling him his calls were no longer expected, and he came to see me. We had a talk over the matter, and agreed to nothing more than friends and we always were friends. He was a good boy but, like myself, didn't have much of this world's goods, but that wouldn't have been in the way if the true love had existed. He failed to get the blonde, after all.

Now, I was in my last term of school. "I must make as much of it as possible. I will be seventeen my birthday and before the next term, I will be over age." I learned fast during the time I was in school, but the terms were so short I never realized that I had accomplished as much as I did, but it is all I ever got. I always regretted that I hadn't the opportunity for an education. I craved book knowledge, and do yet. I could be interested in anything. I could gain knowledge from anything. Anyone could at my age. When school closed, I worked at my quilts and played my violin. Julia and her husband would visit us very often. He was a jolly, good fellow; loved sport, like all the frontier boys. If he had a chew of tobacco and a square meal ahead, he was the happiest man on earth. He went to every dance and pranced all night long; came home next morning full of vim. We never knew what refinement was; all for a good time, but kept within the bounds of reason.

In August there was given a dance and supper by the cowboys at John Flemming's, a ranchman fifteen miles from our home. I wanted to go, but Joe and John were both gone. Levi was the largest brother at home. I did not feel right to go with my beau and just Levi, so Jim lived with my oldest sister and brother-in-law, John Hall, and John's sister wanted to go, so they rigged up a wagon and us five went in the wagon; John's brother and sister and myself and two brothers, Levi and Jim. I felt like I was doing wrong to go, as Joe and John were both away from home. It was a dreadful, rough road and Belle and myself took the back spring seat. Just before we got to the house, we crossed a ditch and, as the hind wheels came out of the ditch, our seat turned over backward, wedging us between the hind gate of the wagon and spring seat. Our head and feet up and fast, too, we called to the boys and Dave, Belle's brother, stopped the wagon and helped us out. Oh, I felt horrid over my predicament.

We soon drove up to the house and got out and went in. The house was crowded with young people and the strains of violin music and the glittering lights filled my heart with inexpressible thoughts. Such a nice smooth floor to dance on and so much room, for it was a nice ranch residence. I met several of my old friends there. Among them was an idiotic kind of a fellow, Jim McBowin. He had tried to court me from the age of thirteen, but I never could bear the old crank. So, the dance went on until ten o'clock, then all took supper as they chose and at anytime they chose. Oh, such a gay time! The table was loaded with all luxuries imaginable. Rebecca and I started to get a drink. As we were just about to pass out the door, I saw Mr. Riley, my old schoolteacher. "How are you, Mr. Riley?" I said.

He arose, walked to me, took hold of my hand and said, in a thick-tongued tone, "Why, Sarah, God bless you," and threw his arms around my neck. Gracious me, if I didn't pitch and jerk loose and run. Oh, I felt that I was disgraced forever.

I ran out of the house and thought to remain out, but the

girls came out from the dining room and got me. Old Jim McBowin was the first man to try to reconcile me. He said, "Whor did he teach you at, Miss Sallie? Whor did he teach you at? You just come on. You got lots of friends. We just put him out the house." I didn't know what to do, but John Flemming soon came in and got me to go back in the house. He said he was drunk, and no one would think the less of you. "I took him out of the house and, if he misbehaves anymore, I'll put him in a room and lock him up."

I finally went in. A young man stepped up to me and got the pleasure of dancing the next set with me. I took the floor, but never enjoyed it, for my mind was on what the people thought of me. I avowed in my mind then, I would never go without Joe or John was with me again. I passed the rest of the night horribly. The dance continued until breakfast; plenty of everything yet on the table for breakfast and all day, if we wanted to dance. One part of the crowd withdrew about ten o'clock.

We had a better trip back. We kept on our guard when we crossed the ditch and kept our balance. When we got home, I pitched against the door and out in the middle of the floor I came, sprawling. There was a neighbor boy.

"Are you drunk?" he said.

"Yes," I said and went on to my oven, put the lid on and succeeded in preparing dinner. All ate but me. I didn't want any. I didn't have any talk for anyone. They soon finished their dinner and were gone; the girls to washing and the young man home, and they didn't get off too quick to please me, either. I wondered all the evening if they knew I was really drunk and what would Joe say if he knew I was drunk. No one ever realized I was drunk but my sisters and John and Dave. It was worth a great deal to me. I never had any more chills, but they did tease me about it when I went back to Sister's. I told John he sure had broke up the chills, but never to tell it on me. He never told it, but I don't see how he kept it, for he was a great tease.

In October, my oldest sister died and left three little children; two little girls and a newborn baby. Oh, it grieved us all so to see three more little orphans added to us. It seemed John Hall could not bear his grief. They put her away by my father and mother, came back home, and his sister took the baby to keep awhile. John said he would keep his little babes at home and do the best he could, but it was only a few days before it seemed unbearable for him and he tried to commit suicide, or was in the act when he was discovered. He had the bottle of strychnine and someone got it and hid it and kept a close watch on him.

Julia and Charley then moved in the house with him and saw after the little girls awhile, but John was very disagreeable, naturally, and they moved out. He brought his baby home as soon as possible, and kept them. Sister Martha stayed with him. She had nursed them all their lives, for Jane kept her and Jim, but Jim was working for himself now. John began to go down in property. At last sold his home and built two little log huts and took Martha and the three little children and moved into them. Martha was only twelve years old. He wouldn't let anyone have them. Oh, he was cranky.

One cold day I felt like I ought to go see how the children were. As I went up, I saw Martha washing, two hundred yards from the house, and John hauling rails. I soon got within hearing of the baby's cries. I went in. There the little thing lay, purple with cold. Jennie, the youngest girl, two years old, was trying to sing and Liza up in a chair with the nurse bottle, trying to fill it with cold milk for the baby, three months old; little Mabin. My heart almost burst. I took him up and warmed and fed him and thought, "What can I do? He won't let me have him." I said, "John, the baby will die if you don't let someone have it."

"No, I'll keep him myself," he said.

I started home and thought of his stepmother (Elizabeth Hall Wood). I went and asked her to try to get John to let her have the baby awhile until she could cure him, for he had laid on his back until the poor little thing was a solid sore. She was kindhearted and very motherly. She went and, after long persuading, he consented to let her have him, but when he called for him, she was to give him up. She became attached to him and loved him as her own. She kept him three years, went to New Mexico with him, stayed nine months, and when she went back to Texas, John tore him from her and let his sister have him. She kept the girls, too.

Chapter 11

My Brothers Return Home

MY BROTHERS NOW ARE at home and Joe has returned to stay. John will work at his old trade with the cowboys, in and out again. Our farm has lain idle ever since Joe joined the Rangers Company. Our horses had all been taken but old Charley, my father's saddle horse, which Joe kept with him all the time he was out. We all loved him as one of the family and he loved us, as well; so much so, he walked in the house one night on Joe's return home to be with the children. It was warm weather and they were all sleeping on the floor on pallets. He walked in among them, giving them a dreadful scare, but was careful not to step on anyone, smelled over them and walked out. Now he is all Joe had of the eleven horses with my father's brand. He concluded he would cultivate our farm, so he goes to work, breaks his land in the spring, put out his crop and soon began to look promising. We had our garden, everything looking nice, and began to have vegetables to eat for the first time since my mother died. I now felt like we could all be much happier.

At night we would amuse ourselves playing the violin. While I cleared away the supper dishes, Joe would play *Old Black Joe*, his favorite piece, lefthanded over the bass. He would begin playing and singing, "I am coming. I am coming. My head is bending low, the voice of the angels calling old black Joe." With a meditating heart full of sad thoughts, I took in the strains of the music. I can now recall his countenance and our situation; too sad to allow my mind to dwell on. He played very smooth with distinct notes and made it so melancholy to me. When I had finished my work, he always handed me the violin. "Here, Sis, play some while I go to sleep." He then retired. I would begin playing and play for hours after all were in bed, sound asleep. I would close by singing and playing, "I love Jesus. Yes, I do. I do love Jesus. He's my saviour. Jesus smiles and loves me, too."

Our hopes of a crop soon vanished. It turned off very dry and the crop was soon burned up. Then Joe had to look out for a job and it was hard to find at that time of the year and on the frontier, too. There was no industry to speak of in those days on the frontier, except stock raising and the spring work was over, so he concluded he would try buying a load of peaches and try his luck peddling. We were soon going to be in another close place again. So, he bought a load from John Flemming, paying him fifty cents per bushel, and started to Concho, which was over a hundred miles away. He wasn't thinking of them ripening so fast and before he got there, they were all in a jelly. He made a complete failure of that, so he came back all out of courage.

The next thing he thought of was a sheep ranch fifteen miles above on the head of Richland Creek. "I'll go see if I can't get to shear sheep." It was shearing time and Bacon & Plants had several thousand to shear. So, he saddled old Charley and set out on Sunday morning and got back that night. "Well, Sis, I got me a job shearing sheep. I never have sheared any, but I can learn how. If anybody can make money at shearing, I can. I will get five cents per head and my board." So, on Monday morning he set out and was gone two weeks. The first trip he made, he had learned to be an expert shearer. He had made several dollars and hadn't fairly begun. He continued to shear until the whole flock was sheared. He made enough money to carry us through the winter very scantily, but we never suffered as we had before.

I had, by this time, given my hand and heart to be married to a young man without an education. He was of a good family and high standing, a son of Pony Hall, but I couldn't see how the children were to get along when I left. I lost no time in making bed clothes and all things necessary for them as Joe could provide me with material. Joe pitched another crop, but only a failure again. He worked at anything he could get to do until sheep shearing again, then set in again and stayed with it until completed. I kept busy making quilts and quilting them. I would help the Browns quilt to get help back. I have helped quilt the odd quilts for them. I began quilting as early as possible in the spring of 1875, for I knew when I left the little ones, they would have a harder time than ever.

Martha was still living with John Hall, so I began to try to persuade her to come home, but I could not have any influence over her. I got Aunt Nancy Harkey to go talk to her and John, too, but it didn't seem to do any good. After several weeks, John decided it was best for her to come home. He went to see an old lady to see if she could keep his two little girls and she agreed to keep his little girls. Then he told Martha it was best for her to come home to me and the other children. She agreed to come, at a word from John, so he brought her home in June 1875. She didn't like to obey me very well, but did it without much trouble. She had been away for six years and it didn't seem like home to her. John was a good provider for his house and she knew we had been almost finished for food oftentimes. John would take us in and give us food and was always kind to her, and she didn't know whether she would fare so well at home or not. We didn't starve, but didn't live very sumptuously.

I never had told Joe my intention of getting married. He was very refined, in his way, and thought I deserved a polished husband when I got married. I knew my circumstances were such that it was impossible for me ever to be thrown among polished young men, living on the frontier as I was. I knew Joe was in love with a grass widow at McKavil and her with him. I studied it all over and I knew it was time I was thinking of a home of my own.

Dave was a very quiet young man and liked by everyone that knew him. He was of a dark complexion, heavy-set and strongly built, with a fierce unfathomable expression, very slow to speak unless aroused to anger, while I was the entire reverse. I had dark hair and light blue eyes, fair skin and a slender form and very small frame, only weighing 115 pounds, while his weight was 157 to 160 pounds. He was five-foot six-inches, while I stood five-foot two-inches. His father died when he was fifteen years old. He left a wife with six children and five stepchildren; his father being a widower when he married Dave's mother. At his death, he owned a large stock of cattle and horses, which he requested that Nathan, his oldest son by his first wife, should control until all the last set was educated and of age. Dave was the oldest son of the last set and had lived in the woods from a small boy with his father's sheep until his father sold them and invested in cattle, for fear he would be picked up by the Indians. Afterward, he became a cowboy and knew nothing but a cowboy's life. Nathan used him for a cowboy ever afterward. Consequently, he had no education when the youngest children came of age. The property was to be divided equally among his wife and eleven children.

Nathan was full of energy and would skin a flea for its hide and tallow, and was very much loved by his stepmother and all the children, but she told the old man when he made his request that Nathan would not deal fairly with her and her children. He replied, "Nathan will give to you and your little ones, rather than take from you." So, that made things all right with her.

Nathan soon began driving herd after herd of cattle to New Mexico and had a fine ranch on the Cimmaron River. The Halls were wealthy people at this time. Dave helped drive and gather and knew as well what belonged to them as Nathan did, for he was almost grown when they drove the last herd. He had a brand of his own and drove them out too, and Nathan was making them rich, fast. So, his stepmother and her children remained in Texas and, after a few years, married Capt. Riley Wood and he bought John Hall's home at the Springs, now known as Richland Springs. It was just a mile west of my native home and Belle and I became very great friends; a sweeter girl never lived. She thought Dave and I were engaged, yet I never told her. I was under the impression Dave had plenty, so I toiled away at home, doing the best I could under the circumstances.

In July I took the chills again. Belle and her mother would come to see me very often and Dave visited us, too. I fared better now, for Martha was with me. When Joe came home from sheep shearing, he bought me chill tonic and broke them up. Then I took the sore eyes and had to keep secluded from the light for three weeks. So many nights I have had one of my little brothers to lead me to the cow lot and milk warm milk in my eyes. It would give them ease for awhile. I would have poultices made of different kinds, but it seemed my eyes would burst out, in spite of all I could do. They finally got well. I was alright for awhile and had a fine time.

Summer nights were very warm and it made it so pleasant to make my bed in the south door on the floor, since a north door caused a draft through the house. Charley and Julia were staying a few days with us and they were sleeping out doors. I had been quilting so much of late, I began dreaming of quilting and the quilting frames falling on me. I was making a dreadful noise and it woke Julie. She had Charley come to the door to see what was ailing me. He called to me to know what was the matter. I told him nothing, but I was sound asleep. He went back to bed. The quilting frames kept falling on me and I kept up my distressing noise. She sent him back and told him to go to me. He called to me again, asking me what was the matter.

I was sitting up in bed. I said, "I believe a polecat has bit me." It excited him, for they are dangerous. I was still asleep, sitting in bed.

He spoke in an excitable tone, "Where is it?"

I said, "Here it is"; still asleep.

"Where?" he asked.

"Here in my hand," and as I handed it to him, I awoke. I had it by the back of the neck. That was the quilt that was falling on me. It had bitten me seven times, and it had chewed my right little finger into a pulp, and bit through the joint where the finger joins the hand, and on the elbow, and twice on the muscle between the elbow and shoulder, and through the upper lip, then nailed to my nose between the nostrils. That is when I clinched it by the back of the neck. Charley threw it out in the yard. For all we handled it, there was no scent of a skunk left. The cat got away through the excitement over me being bitten.

Oh, my, I was excited, almost into a nervous fit; Charley and Julia, too. We all dressed and went to Mamma Brown's to have her doctor the bites. I wanted her to put gunpowder on the bites and touch it off. I heard my father tell of a man being bitten while on an Indian scout and they put gunpowder to the bite and touched it off. That was all I knew to do for my wounds, but she didn't approve of my suggestion. She applied turpentine and salt and the yolk of an egg to the wounds. We then went back home and I soon got over my scare and thought but little about it, but Julia was very uneasy. She knew of a man that was in possession of a mad stone, Nat Johnson, who lived on the head of the Brady Creek, thirty miles away. She consulted Captain Wood's wife about sending for the stone. They decided to send for it, so Charley lost no time in going after it.

Belle came down to spend the day with us. Along about ten o'clock in the morning, I began to feel stupid and bad. My arm ached to my shoulder and I said, "Belle, let's take a walk and maybe I'll feel better." I didn't know Charley had gone for the mad stone. Julia had said nothing to me about it and I didn't know anyone was uneasy about me. As to my part, I never thought of it being serious, although I had a taste in my mouth I never had had before. It seemed to taste like a dog's breath smells. We walked about the bluff for some time and finally I said, "Belle, let's go down to the water. My hand and arm pains me so. I'll put it in the water and I think it will help to reduce the fever and likely relieve it." We walked down the ledge of rock to the water. I sat down and, just as I turned to put my hand into the water, a strange feeling came over me. "Oh, Belle, I do feel so strange. Let's go to the house"; not knowing hydrophobia could be tested by water. We went to the house, but I said nothing of my strange feeling.

I continued to feel worse and worse. After dinner Julia told me Charley had gone for the mad stone, but I felt so bad I thought but little about it. At two o'clock that evening he came with the stone. It was a small, flat, dark colored stone, almost square, and slick and smooth, as if it had been dressed. It was about one and one-fourth-inches long and three-fourths inches wide and one-eighth of an inch thick, and the man said to apply the narrow edge to the wound. It didn't look possible it could adhere to anything with the narrow edge. It must be soaked in warm, sweet milk first and taken out and dried thoroughly, then applied while warm. Charley said, "If it adheres, there is poison. If not, there is no danger." So, they prepared the stone according to Mr. Johnson's instructions. It stuck like a leech until full of poison, then it dropped off. They dropped it back into the sweet milk and let it be until the poison soaked out. Then dried it and applied again, and so on, for three days and nights. We could see the poison rise on the milk like small, green beads. Such a breath I had and such dead sleep I slept, and so queer I would feel at times, but it gradually left me as the poison was extracted from my system.

Joe came in from his work in a day or so, awfully surprised to think we were so fortunate to get the stone, and felt so thankful. "We must send this stone home," he said, for fear we would get it broken. Johnson was very careful with it and cautioned Charley very particular about it, so Joe sent it back with many thanks to Mr. Johnson for his kindness, but I never felt as well afterward. In the course of two weeks, Mr. Johnson was passing down through our country and he stopped with us a few minutes. He told Joe he ought to have kept the stone and on the ninth day applied again. This, he said, was the proper way to have used it and then there would never be any danger afterward. The bites affected me for twenty-seven years, at times, but I never feel the effects anymore. I had begun to have rosy cheeks before the cat bite but now the color began to fade away and it was nearing my wedding day.

Joe went off to work and I continued to rake and scrape all the children's clothing and mend them; it now being about the middle of August. I had, by now, plenty of covers for winter. Joe would, at times, speak to me about D.C., as he always called Dave, to try to lead me out about whether we were intending to get married. I would tell him something about my intentions, as he always showed me his letters from his widow. He would say, "Sis, I don't see how I could get along if you was to get married. I just can't keep house without you." I knew Dave was not his choice for me and I would say, "Oh, I am not married yet by quite a good deal and, besides, there is scarcely a young man of my acquaintance that is competent to make a good husband," but I knew Dave was very kind to his mother and sister and felt like that was good evidence he would be kind to me.

His mother and Belle were very foolish about him, as he was the oldest brother and never would stay away from home long at a time. His mother and stepfather didn't agree very well, there being four sets of children between them. Captain Wood had been married three times and had four children by each of his first two wives and she had six children and five stepchildren, but none by the Captain. Such a mixed family naturally will disagree, and she confided a great deal in Dave. Consequently, he never would stay away from her long at a time. The older boys had Mid and Susan, their half brother and sister, with them and put them in school at Trinidad, Colorado. Martha, Dave's oldest sister, was married to Warren Hudson and his baby brother, Oliver, lived with Martha, and Belle lived with her mother the greatest part of her time, and Dave lived at his mother's and Martha's. He would often say to me in our conversations, "I'll tell you, we are liable to have to live hard when we are married." I thought he seemed worried and seemed to dread the idea of getting married, but I would say, "I don't feel uneasy at all of hard times," but it made me feel as though he was dissatisfied with me. He assured me he was not in the least dissatisfied with me.

So, time drifted nearer to the appointed day, which was the third day of October. Joe was not at home very much, only coming in when his job ended and staying until he found another, so I knew he would be in on Saturday before we were to get married on Sunday at two o'clock in the afternoon. I had invited all my friends to our marriage. The ceremony was to be performed by our County Justice, John Gannery, at the home of the bride at two o'clock in the afternoon on the third day of October 1875. I was now into my twentieth year, since the 2nd of March, and Dave into his twenty-fourth year, since the 2nd of May.

On Saturday night, Joe came home, sure enough, but I never told him until the next morning. He was so displeased at me going to get married and said Dave was not suited for me at all. He said I could do better than to take him. Oh, he was all worked up. "I am going to leave right now," he said. "I won't stay to see you married."

Oh, my, I was cut to the heart. I began to cry and talk to him. "Why, Joe, you never did say you disregarded Dave in the least, and he has been paying his respects to me nearly two years. Why didn't you say something long ago? Now, I don't want you to leave and it is no use for you to be angry with me now." So, that ended our conversation. He soon reconsidered the matter and remained at home.

There was an old lady and gentleman living in our neighborhood; Uncle Caleb Jones and Aunt Vinie. I had them to come and stay all day. They came early Sunday morning. I did hope to have beautiful sunshine and a mild day and when the sun rose that morning, it never was so bright and brilliant, before or since, to me, but in a few hours it began to turn a little cool. I kept a close watch and after a while there began to show dim streaks of clouds and by two o'clock, the appointed hour, the skies were streaked with thin clouds and a very mild breeze was blowing.

The guests were all there awaiting the groom. At two o'clock sharp, they cried, "He is coming." My heart leaped and thumped, almost choking me. A second later, my brother led him in and seated him by my side. The Justice of the Peace was an Englishman. I had known him as a small child but never could understand him very well, but, on this occasion, I wanted to understand every word he said, for I never pledge myself to anything before knowing what it is. Consequently, I was steady nerved when we were pronounced man and wife.

Chapter 12

Sailing Out on the Voyage of Matrimony

IN A FEW HOURS the guests all took their departure. Dave owned a fine yoke of oxen and loaned them to a friend of his to use, as he had no use for them and, after all were gone, up drives the man with the oxen. He had been off hauling and heard of the wedding and drove by. So, Dave and my brothers went out to where he was. They talked quite a little while and the man drove on. I heard Joe say, "Dave, I swear he has just beat you out of your oxen. That wagon is well worn out and your steers are fine steers."

"I believe I'll rue the trade, but I need the wagon now," he said.

"Yes," says the boys, "but that wagon is no good."

So, he overtook the man and tried to rue, but he knew a good thing when he had it in his fingers. So, the next morn he got his horse and one for me to ride and saddled them up, and we went to his mother's.

Oh, my, the wind blew so hard I could hardly sit in the saddle. After we got there I had a dumb chill, but tried not to complain. Oh, I felt wretched. He made arrangements with his stepfather and mother to live there two months and all was agreed to. Riley, as he called his stepfather, complimented Dave highly and said, "Dave, you have got the pick of the county for a

71

wife. Now, if you will do your part, you will do well." He made no reply. I felt like he ought at least to thank him, yet he meant no harm in his silence.

So, on Wednesday he hitched old Dock, a big brown horse, and old Dan, a big sorrel horse, to his old, run down wagon he traded for and we went after my little possessions, which consisted of a feather bed, two small pillows, one quilt, two quilt tops ready to quilt, and my clothes. After he got them in the wagon, we were talking with Joe and the horses got frightened at something and away they went with the wagon and my little belongings. He set out in a run to head them off, as they had to make a turn when they struck the bluff to get out. I thought he would kill himself running. That was all I was interested in. The horses, wagon, and my belongings never entered my mind, but he headed them and got them stopped and nothing hurt, so he drove back to the house. I left all my quilts I had made for Joe and the children. I felt like I could make more and they couldn't. So, we got in our wagon and started, leaving them all alone. I could see Joe was hurt to the bottom of his heart. We got home safe and sound.

In the course of a month, I began to be troubled with rheumatism, which gave me no little pain, and Dave was gone to his sister's more than I thought he ought. I needed to quilt some and had no cotton. He went to shear the black sheep in his mother's flock with which I was to pad my quilts with the wool. It seemed to me I could have sheared the whole flock in the time he put in shearing the black ones. I began to feel like he neglected me and didn't return the love due me, for I loved him very dearly.

He came home from Martha's, his sister, where he had been to shear sheep, and came where I was. I was so anxious to see him but he seemed so unconcerned, as though he never had been gone. Oh, my, it struck me deep to my heart. I thought, "He doesn't care to be with me. He would rather be with his mother and sisters." He never had any conversation for me at any time. It grieved me deeply. I said to Belle, "What makes Dave do me as he does? It seems as he is mad toward me."

"Oh, Sallie, that is Dave's ways. He was always that turn," she said. I was so disappointed in his disposition, I couldn't give it up that it was his ways.

He finally came in where I was and said to me, "You will have to go stay with Martha awhile. She is not able to do her work."

"Me? No, I won't either," I said.

"Well, Belle will have to go then," he said.

Oh, it shot like a dagger to my heart. Here I am not well at all and him wanting me to go wait on his sister. I thought, "Now, if he had said, 'we will go stay with Martha awhile,' it would have delighted me," but for me to go alone, it hurt me.

"Well," said he, "You may want someone to stay with you sometime."

I replied, "If I did, she wouldn't stay with me." So, that stopped our conversation. We almost had cross words in such a short time. I thought him my shield and protector and him wanting me to go to work. Oh, it pierced me like a knife. Then I began to grieve secretly and, of course, it showed on me.

When the two months were up, we moved just a little distance from his mother's. I soon found out he would pout if anything went wrong. So, when things didn't go right, he stayed at his mother's for his meals. I stayed at home and grieved and never said anything to him about it, yet, it grieved me all the time.

I never had been to see the children since we left on Wednesday, after we were married. I would try to get him to go with me, but he never would go. Oh, I was bothered over his ways. He always seemed as though he couldn't make a living and I couldn't see why that bothered him. I felt like he was sorry he had married me. I always was very affectionate and he was very distant, not showing his affection, no matter how much he loved one.

So, time passed along until Christmas day. There was going to be a dance at Flemmings that night. Belle and I wanted to go but Dave didn't, so he got on his horse and rode off to Martha's. Brother John came to my house around twelve. It was a very warm day for Christmas and we had no fire at all in the fireplace. Belle was there, too, and we all agreed to go home with her for dinner. After dinner we saw a man running toward our house and John, looking, saw our house in smoke. I ran, too. When I got there they were dragging out my feather bed with the tick burned off and the feathers flowing out. All I had was burned up.

There was a thick mesquite thicket northwest of the house and the next morning I saw I could gather quite a lot of feathers up that had drifted about the roots of the bushes. So, Belle and I went to work. I picked and cried. After awhile, Joe came up and, seeing me crying, laughed and said, "Sis, are you picking geese out there?" That almost killed me. I wanted his sympathy, for I was as bad as if I had lost a fortune. It was all I had; just as bad as if I had been worth hundreds of dollars and lost it. The fire had caught from a spark out of a young man's pipe, as he went out at the door, when we started over to Riley's just before dinner. Now, I was completely broken up. All I had was burned up; nothing left but my few head of hogs I had raised from pet pigs Jasper Brown had given me, and Dave was out of humor with me, too. That was troubling me deeply. So, John Hall loaned me a mattress and Belle loaned me a quilt and I took the black wool and made me a comfort and, in a few weeks, John moved his whole plunder into the house with me and his two little girls. The house was saved. It being an old log house, they soon put out the fire. So, now we did fairly well, yet Dave's ways worried me no little, and kept me in deep wonder. I couldn't understand him and I had always said if I ever got married I never would quarrel with my husband.

The last of January, Nath and his wife came in and brought Susan home. He had accumulated a great wealth out in New Mexico. Him and two of his brothers, William and Jim, being equal partners, leaving John, an own brother, and his stepmother and her children out. He brought an instrument of writing in for them to sign, paying them one hundred dollars for their interest in their father's estate. He had Susan's name and Mid's already signed. He came over and took Dave out and presented his document and asked him to sign it and he would then pay him one hundred dollars for his interest in the estate. Dave had known their scheme for quite a while, but he never had told me anything about it. His anger was aroused to a considerable pitch and he refused to sign the document; also posted his mother not to sign it. He told Nath he knew what belonged to him and if he didn't give him his just rights, he would never sign his name to a paper showing he had value received for his just rights, of which he had slaved for from a very small boy, and all his own personal property, too. This great wrong in Nath caused a deep-seated anger in Dave's heart toward his three half-brothers, so when Dave told me about it, then I knew why he seemed so bothered. So, now I knew we were in a poverty-stricken condition, but I had been in poverty so long it didn't strike me deep like it did him. He went about very glum, not knowing what he was to do.

In February, Joe got in the hogs to kill and my hogs were fat,

Amy Hall Warren (right), Sarah's oldest daughter,
with husband Louis Thomas Warren and their only child, Beulah.

Dee Hall, Sarah's next to youngest.

D. R. (Dee) Harkey, Sarah's brother, author of Mean As Hell.

Left: *Minor Hall, Sarah's youngest child.*

Right: *Matthew Hall, second child of Sarah and David.*

Tree in which Sarah hid from Indians, Richland Springs.
From left, Tana Gray, Jada Brazell, Jan Brazell,
Maridell Lambert Henry, and Beulah Lambert.

too; got fat on oak mash. We went down and killed all but one. He was not with the bunch and had strayed off. Now we had our meat for the year. We thought four hogs ought to run us quite awhile. Dave finally decided he would put in a farm across the county, nine miles north of Richland on Wilbargo Creek, on a tract of R.R. land; a fine piece of land, too. He said he could buy it at fifty cents per acre, so he set out to work, leaving me with John and the two little girls. I was very poor in health. After a few weeks I took very sick, terminating in a case of abortion; bothering him quite a good deal in his progress toward clearing his ground.

After I recovered, we took a family in the house with us from Missouri that was in a destitute condition. John had taken his little girls to an old lady and left me enough bedding to make out on. So, Mrs. Adams and I became very great friends. I loved her as a sister and Dave and Billy Adams, her husband, were like brothers. What one had, the other got their share.

At that time, buffalo hunters were on the western plains, killing buffalo and drying the meat and speculating it, having it hauled down in the eastern counties and selling it at a fair price. Dave, being acquainted with the speculation, contracted to haul several loads. So, he let Billy have a load to haul and Dave Adams, Bill's brother, wanted a load, too; he being in the same condition as his brother. So, he let them both have a load. They were fresh from the old countries; never had seen a buffalo, and when they got out to the plains, they saw a buffalo calf making for their wagons. Dave stopped his team and Billy stopped, too. Old Dave Adams said, "What have we stopped for?"

Dave said, "That calf will take right to our teams and my horses will tear everything loose."

So, Old Dave said, "Oh, the devil, I'll drive on. My mules won't notice it."

"You had better stop, I tell you, your mules will tear things to pieces," Dave said.

"Oh, the devil, you say," said Old Dave, and drove on.

When the calf came up grunting and hugged up to his mules, they went to kicking and pitching and running and falling. After awhile, they kicked loose and around and around they went. The old man took in after them, finally caught the calf, and knocked it in the head. Dave and Billy burst their sides laughing at him. They had to hold their own teams and couldn't assist the old man. When he got the calf killed and caught his team, he lit in on Dave and Billy, mad as a wet hen, for not helping him. They teased him for being so bold.

The next day, as they drove along, they saw, off to one side of the road, a large buffalo lie down. Old Dave was delighted at the thought of killing a buffalo, so they agreed to slip up as near as possible, all stop and count three, and then fire. They were slipping along and Dave saw that Old Dave had slipped off his shoes. "What did you pull off your shoes for?" asked Dave.

"What do you reckon, but to run," said Old Dave.

They got as near as possible, Dave forgetting what he had said about running, and they counted three and fired. The buffalo got up, wounded. Two shots had struck him, so Dave was telling Old Dave and Billy to not move and let the buffalo see them and they would get him the shot. He looked around and Old Dave was sifting sand toward the wagon like a scared wolf. Dave killed the buffalo and left him lying and went on to where they had started, loaded their wagons, and started home. After getting home, Billy and Dave agreed to let Old Dave Adams haul it to market and divide the profit when he got back. He pulled out east and Dave and I got a tent and moved to our farm.

We lived in a tent all that summer. In the fall, Dave built a log house and moved into it. Through the summer we palleted down on quilts and beef hides and my thin feather bed I had gathered after the burn. While he built our log hut, brother Jim and Oliver and I pulled grass and I made a bed and a pair of pillows. I was alright now for beds.

As we failed to raise a crop, we were in a dreadful, close place, yet I never suffered any uneasiness of starving. We had one neighbor, Mr. Roberts. Every little while, Dave would go down and get a quarter of a beef. I never thought anything about it and thought it was alright, which it was; for at that time, there was lots of wild, fat cattle. They would wait until the cattle would come in at night to water, then they would shoot one. You never would see one in daytime. There was nothing thought of anyone killing out the wild cattle to get rid of them.

During this time, Julia sent my brother after me. She was not well, so Dave told me to go stay with her a week or so. So, I went, but in a few days I had a distressing feeling come over me that Dave was sick. I couldn't get rid of my distressing feeling. Since

Julia was not able to be alone, I insisted they move to the springs, nearer where we lived. I succeeded in moving them to the springs. We got in just before dark. Just after dark, one of my brothers trailed us up. Dave was dying, he said. They had been trying to find me all day. So few people lived in the county, no one knew of us moving from the mouth of the creek back to the springs. He had diphtheria and was dying when he left. He had come over to a lady doctor. She lived four miles below the springs. I got up behind Levi on his horse and lost no time in going. When I got there, he was better. As soon as he recovered, we went back home.

It was getting late in the fall and I had very little bedding for winter. We heard of my hog that had strayed off and he was fat. I knew that Dave could not buy anything, as he hadn't a cent of money, so I told him to sell my hog. If he could get $5 for him, I could buy material to make sufficient bedding to go through the winter. So, he did and, as we lived on the road to San Saba, I watched my chance to send for my material. The first man passing was a Mr. Ford. I told him what I wanted; a pair of cotton cards, material for comforts, and the balance in cotton.

"Will you be so kind as to bring them out for me?" I asked.

"Certainly, I will," he said.

The day following, I got my material. I went to work and soon had my comforts made and a nice mattress. I felt rich enough for anyone.

During this time, Joe had married [a] widow and the children didn't like her. Levi had left him and come to me. He was now fifteen years old. He helped Dave all he could, but we were so poverty-stricked, he hadn't much to do. Feeling he was working an imposition on us, he concluded he would go down east with Julia and Charley.

John came in now and made our house his home. He would visit the children often. So, he made them a visit and came home very wroth [sic] at Joe and his wife. He said Joe had punished my little sister just to please his wife. I never had complained at anything Joe did, but this aroused me considerable. I sent her word if she ever did cause Joe to whip Annie again without a cause, I would mix it with her, for I knew Annie was such an innocent child she didn't deserve such punishment.

In a day or two, Joe came over to see me about what I had

said. "I heard, Sis, you were mad at Henrietta about me punishing Annie," he said.

"Yes. I don't intend she shall have my little brother and Annie beaten like dogs. I never had to beat them and I know, if she treats them right, they won't need very much chastisement. I just won't stand it. That is the wood with the bark on it," I said.

He twisted his mustache awhile, in deep thought. "Well, Sis, you can have her. I think you ought to have her," he said.

I was glad to get her; just ten years old the next June she would be. I never felt that I ought to say anything to Dave in regard to taking her, which would have been proper in me to have consulted him. I sent after her right then and, in a short time, Eli, the baby, seven years old, came to us. If I hadn't the biggest-hearted man in the world, he would have made a racket about it, but it was alright with him. I still didn't understand his ways. They were so different to what I thought his ways to be, but he traded and trafficked around and made a living for us all; never talking scarcely any. I would think he was pouting. I was the reverse; talking and laughing if I could get anyone to talk to. As he would say, I would talk if the world was coming to an end.

In 1877, January 30, our first child was born; a fine boy, a very promising child. Dave was very proud of him, but I was left in such wretched health. I was confined to my bed six weeks with the physician coming every day. The little babe took seriously ill at seven days old. We both lingered along. I, at last, got out of bed, but pale as death. Poor little Annie had such a hard time, but never faltered or complained at anything. A nobler child never lived. Being in debt so, Dave sold his improvement to a man for two wagons and three work horses to traffic on. He soon sold one of the horses to a Norwegian for $20 in money. It sure looked big to me.

By this time, Mid had come back from New Mexico. He had some clear cash and he bought a piece of land and a small bunch of cattle. He built a log hut on his land and got Dave to move on his place and keep his cattle. He would assure him the place for five years and, if he would put in a farm, he could have all he could make. So, it was a trade.

The baby was now seven weeks old, but still sick. Dave got my brother, Jim, to borrow a hack to move me and the babe over in. I was pale as death; not able to care for the baby. Annie was all my stay. A sweeter child never lived. Dave was as kind as he knew how to be, but he knew but very little how a wife should be cared for, being raised astride a horse and in the woods. He really was ignorant of a husband's duty altogether. This being the case, I was very much troubled, besides all my infirmities and my sick baby to trouble over. I was ignorant of all his worries. He was undergoing the debts hanging over him and no way out he could see at that time. He had nothing but his team and the two wagons and two ponies to trade on. He had a bunch of shoats, too. He got a bunch of pigs of his stepfather's to raise on the shares, as we had lots of mast all around us. I have thought, so often, about his condition along those days; an invalid wife and baby and my sister and from two to three of my brothers to support in his condition of poverty. Not one out of a hundred would have bore it. He was kind to my sister and brothers always, but still I felt he didn't return the kindness to me that I felt was due me.

Thus, I dwindled along; Annie and Dave making preparations to move. So, on the 13th of March 1877, he set to move to Mid's place. The baby seemed better and it was warm that morning. The buds had begun to swell for a new spring and the air was filled with the sweet odor of plum blooms, yet my spirit could not revive within me. I had a sad, heavy heart all morning. At twelve, all was loaded and ready to start. Jim soon drove up in the hack. I didn't think the baby was as well as it seemed that morning, but we were ready to go and thought we had better go on. So, I wrapped the babe and soon was ready to go.

I got in and took the babe and Dave told Jim to drive through with the baby and me; not to wait for him. He would be on as soon as possible. Jim drove fast, for I saw the baby was growing worse fast. I kept Annie with me. When we had gone about four miles, I saw the baby had a spasm. "Oh, Jim, stop." He did so. We waited until it passed off, then drove on again, losing no time. It took another spasm, then we stopped again and waited until the spasm passed away. We then drove very slowly the rest of the way, getting there about an hour by sun in the afternoon. He got out and helped us out and we went in the house and he soon made a fire. The baby seemed very stupid, but had no more spasms.

In a short time, Dave drove up. They soon unloaded our scanty household plunder and Annie prepared our supper. After eating, Jim went on horse guard, as he was working for Jim Hall, and he was ready to start to his ranch on the Cimmaron in a week or ten days. The baby remained very stupid all night, not nursing any at all through the night.

When day began to break, Annie awoke and prepared breakfast. All had eaten but me. I sat and nursed my suffering babe. As they had done with their breakfast, Jim went to his herd and Dave and Annie were busy arranging. I still sat holding the little babe, looking down upon it with a young mother's sympathy. When it seemed to gape, I rubbed my hand over its face to make it catch its breath but, lo, the spirit had taken its flight to the realms of bliss. I called to Dave. He rushed in. It was dead. I closed its eyes and sent for Jim's wife and Dave's sister, Martha. They dressed and prepared him for burial.

The next day we were going to lay his little remains to rest. When the time came for the funeral procession to start, I had not sufficient clothes to wear so Martha helped me out in this respect, and we laid our dear babe to rest in the cemetery where my parents were buried and turned homeward with a sad heart.

Chapter 13

Three Years in the Log House

NOW, WE ARE HERE in a newly made home of Dave's brother with cows to give milk, which was a great thing to us. Warren Hudson, Martha's husband, had kept the little flock of sheep of Dave's mother for several years, and now he was going to move to New Mexico with Jim's horses. So the sheep were turned over to Dave. Warren had several hives of bees and he needed a tent, so Dave traded our tent for his bees. One of the flies being torn off, Dave brought it to me to sew back on. I worked a half day, hard, to finish it. I really was not able to do anything. When he came in after it, he saw I had sewed it in upside down. I was already irritated over my half day's work and he got worried at me for doing my work wrong and ordered me to rip it out and do it over; whereupon, I lost my temper and told him I would not sew another stitch. I felt like he was imposing on me and, of course, he got mad and we had a few cross words, but I never ripped my work out. Those were the first cross words we ever had. So, that soon passed over.

He made his trade with the tent for his bees. In a few days they were to start. Now, Dave had heard of a few head of scattered remnant cattle of their father's brand. He went to Jim to get his consent to gather them and Jim gave him his interest in the remnant, also said he would get the other two boys to give him their interest. We were just about as poor as Job's turkey and he had to lean against the fence to gobble. We were glad to get anything, although I hadn't failed to have a square meal since we married.

Now, brother Jim was going to New Mexico with Hall's horses and then remain there on the ranch as a hand, which troubled me to know he would be separated from us for so long; the first one of my brothers to leave home and him only eighteen, except Levi, and he was with Julia. John made my house his home now, so our family was quite large. The children always knew where to find a home. We now had four of them with us; John, Annie, Eli, and Jeff. Joe had Moses and Dee. So, John Hall and children and Hudson and family immigrated to New Mexico.

We, of course, took all their old traps left which helped us out considerable. We now were left behind with a more prosperous future before us. Dave began to rustle after the remnants. All the cowmen were his friends. They always looked out for him and, by that time, he had five cows and calves.

My health continued to grow worse. I was a walking skeleton, confined to my bed most of my time, and the doctor had to be called every few days, but I got no relief. At last, the doctor said it was the cat bite or consumption. He couldn't do me any good by coming to see me, which was very honest in him. We now owed him double and triple what we were worth, but he was very easy with us and would take anything we had on his bill. We had good luck with our bees; had run them up to several hives. The doctor took them and paid a fair price for them and bacon, too. When we had anything to share, it belonged to Dr. Taylor. The little bunch of sheep helped us out wonderfully.

I felt like I was a perfect nuisance. I lay and read the Bible, or tried to. I couldn't make any sense out of it. I knew I couldn't live long and I had a great desire to know what God's promises were to us, that I might prepare myself to meet the great judgment day I had heard my father preach about while I was very small, but the more I read, the more I was confused, not divining the word of God properly.

Dave was more attentive to me now. He stayed by me all he could and John was very kind to me, too. In fact, they were all very anxious about me. At last, one day I was lying on my bed and Dave was sitting by me and it came over me that if I would go to

Mrs. Lindley's, a lady who lived twenty miles above us on the Colorado River, I would get well. She could help me. I said, "Dave, I am going to die if I don't go to Mrs. Lindley's."

"Why? Do you think she could do you any good?" he asked.

"Yes. If I can get to her, I will get up," I said.

"Well, if you want to go, I'll take you," he said.

"How can I ever get there?" I asked.

"I'll borrow a hack and take you," he said.

So, he did and when we got there he told the lady what I had said and asked her what she could do for me.

"I don't know until I examine her," she said. She made an examination and took him to one side and told him she would do all she could for me and said, "But you have put off having her treated too long, I am afraid, but let her remain with me. I will see what I can do for her. You may go home. If she doesn't get along all right, I will let you know. You can come back every few days."

So, in nine days there was a marked change in me, but seemingly for the worse. I knew nothing at all. I frothed at the mouth. She used electric needles on the calves of my legs and, in several hours, I became rational again. She treated me with simple remedies; weak lye baths, cotton seed poultices over the abdomen, and put me on a bitter, she called it. In three weeks, I had improved so much, she said I could go home. So, Dave took me home. The children and one friend were so surprised to see a change for my recovery. Dave and the children cared for me just like a baby and I gradually improved all the summer, but never was well.

During this time, Joe had rented our homeplace out to a widow lady with three boys, two of them young men, and had moved to Kimble County and took Mose and Dee and the cattle that belonged to us all; our father's stock. Sister Martha went east to where Julia was. She was about fifteen years old. Now we were scattered. Oh, it grieved me no little; me being so delicate. I was brewing trouble. I feared the boys might get into serious trouble or in need of my advice, as I had always advised them. I still felt the responsibility. I had always taught them never to let their temper get the better of them and kill someone; to always run. A living coward was better than a dead hero. My whole soul yearned after them. Letter after letter I would write Jim, advising him how to live and how to conduct himself to make an honorable, upright man. I put my soul and strength in my letter to him. As Levi was with Julia, I felt better satisfied about him and John lived with me, so I could talk to him at ease. A nobler-hearted man never lived than John. He always expressed himself openly.

Dave didn't get much land in the first year, only about three acres. John and Jeff helped him some, making rails and fencing and clearing ground. They would help him do anything he asked them to do, for Dave and John were always like brothers; never had a cross word in their life. They always helped to shear sheep.

One instance occurred, while shearing sheep, I'll never forget. We had a shepherd dog that sucked eggs and I wanted John or Dave to kill him, but neither one wanted to kill him. I had a hen sitting on a nest of eggs and Woolie, the dog, broke her up. I went to the sheep pen where they were and told them they just had to kill that dog. They laughed at me and said they wouldn't kill him. "Well, I will," I said.

"There is the shotgun. Go after him."

So, I went and put a rope on his neck and led him off from the house, carrying my gun upon my shoulder. After I got him where he wouldn't be offensive to smell, I tied him to a mesquite. I took up my gun and cocked it and lifted it to blow his head off. Just then, Woolie looked me in the eyes and began to wag his tail. "I will kill you anyway, if you do plead with your eyes and tail," I said. I leveled the gun between his eyes and pulled the trigger. I knew in my mind he would never know what hurt him. Just as the gun fired, I closed my eyes and the dog yelled. I turned, never looking back, and went to the house.

"Now, go back and finish him," the boys said. "You have crippled him."

I never went. After several hours. I told Annie to go see if he was dead and, if he was alive, see if I had crippled him seriously. "If not, bring him to the house."

She went on. After awhile she led him up with the dog wagging his tail.

"Where did I shoot him, Annie? I can't find any place." I looked and I had just burned all the wool off his head and never scratched the hide. That broke me of killing a dog. I never heard the last of that from John. He always teased me about being such a markswoman.

During this time, it was found out it was an evident fact that

Gus Stevenson, a son of the widow lady that lived in our old home, was a horse thief. By chance, John was a very important witness against him, which caused me no little trouble, for I knew from his looks he was very treacherous and I was impressed that he aimed to kill John. I talked so much to him about being so careless. I would tell him Gus was intending to kill him.

"Oh, he won't bother me," he said.

"Oh, I tell you, he will," I said.

"Why, Gus seems to like me," he said.

"I know he does, but he is so treacherous he is going to kill you and you will never know it," I told him.

A short time afterward, we were told that Gus had waylaid the road for John. A few days after, John went to Richland and was coming on home when Gus fell in with him and came on home with him, it being warm weather. We kept a bedstead out in the far corner of the yard. Gus asked John if he slept there. "Yes," said John, "it is a fine place to sleep." After a while, he left; John thinking no harm of his maneuvers, not even telling it. Several days afterward, Andy Baird was there and, in the evening, asked John to go spend the night with him. So, he went. After a few hours, in the night, our dogs ran out like someone was just coming up. I told Dave somebody must be around close, from the way the dogs barked. He picked up the gun and hissed at the dogs. He saw two men run from the corner of the fence where the bed stood. We supposed it to be Gus trying to get in his work on John while he was asleep, but found him gone.

When John came home, I said, "John, I want you to never go out at night anymore. I believe Gus was here last night to kill you in your bed."

"Oh, I am not afraid of him killing me. He is too big a coward," he said.

"Well, I want you to prepare to protect yourself. You never do carry anything to defend your life," I said.

"Oh, pshaw, there is no use in that," he said.

So, it went on. We never heard anything more to the contrary for several months. John went where he pleased with the Lord watching over him, having his sport. He was a fine marksman and would often sport for money that way. He struck a crowd at Milburn, a little burg in McCulloch County, one day and Bud Bradley wanted to shoot with anyone in the crowd, at a spot, for $5. John took him up. Bradley gave him the first shot. He handed John the gun. They put the stakes in Judge Beadey and Shelby Wilson's hands. So, John shot and drove the center and handed the gun to Bud. He just turned and threw the gun on John and demanded stakes. The stake holders, being old friends of John's and our father, too, persuaded him to let him have it. "Alright, then, I'll see him another time." My health was very poorly and this news distressed me. My spirit seemed to be with the boys at all times. I talked with those with me and wrote to those away. Yet, I was not a member of the church.

A couple of weeks after he gave up stakes, John and Andy Baird wanted us to let the few young people dance at our house. So, Dave consented right off, but I hesitated, but finally consented.

Bradley came and as soon as John saw him he said, "I will make him hand over my five dollars this night or I'll have his hide."

Oh, my! I took him in the little pigpen of a kitchen we had and talked and reasoned and pled for my life to him to not molest him, for he had no character and if you deal with such people, you will get the worst of it. After a while, Andy joined me and he said, for my sake, he would drop it. So that dread was unloaded, but I still had a trouble hanging over me.

We were doing very well financially. We had raised some wheat and our wool bought our necessaries. We had goats and could kill a kid and have fresh meat and had plenty of nice honey, and lots of friends, of which I loved best of all. Annie was now getting to be very pretty, I thought. Nothing I had was too good for her, and Eli and her both seemed to love Dave as well as they did me. When he was in the woods and found grapes, plums, pecans, or anything that he thought would please me and the children, he always brought it in to us. They always watched to see him come, to see what he had for them. I never thought much about a living, I had so much confidence in Dave. I felt perfectly free in that respect.

We had considerable rain that year and in the fall we had a water spout at night. We knew it was raining, but that is when people sleep the soundest. Late in the night John awoke and heard the terrible noise. He jumped up and opened the door and when the lightening flashed, there was a sea of water all around us. "Get up, Dave. We are all going to be drowned," he said.

He jumped up and looked out. "By doggy, John, what can we do?"

It was just pouring down rain and heavy thunder roaring and the water dashing in at the door. "Oh, Lord, have mercy on us." I fell upon my knees with supplications of prayers to our Heavenly Father. I had been baptized into Christ a short time before and I put all my trust in the Lord to save us. While I was in supplication to the Lord, John was out trying to find a way of escape to the hills. In a few moments he rushed to the door.

"Dave, get a chair and quilts for Diden (that is a nickname for me) to sit on and to keep her dry and grab a chunk of fire from the fireplace and try and not to let it rain out, and Annie, you hold fast to Dave. Eli you hold to Annie and Diden you get on my back. I've found where we can get out. It is deep, but follow me. I'll carry you out." We went all of a quarter of a mile in water from knee-deep to waist-deep, dark as ever I saw, except when it flashed lightening. He led us on to land. Dave put the chair down and John set me on it and Annie and Eli by me and covered us with quilts. Then he made a fire. It rained the rest of the night.

When the chickens crowed, John and Dave went to see how the water was. It was falling. By daybreak they could go where the house was. They found Andy Baird's mare at the house. They saddled her and brought her out and Annie and I rode in. Nothing was hurt at the house, but our hogs washed off. The rain loosened everything loose about the place.

It was laughable to John after it was over. He went to Brown's and, telling Old Dady about it, said, "Oh, it was frightful. Diden fell to praying and Dave, scared almost to death, said, 'Oh, I wish I could pray! Jerusalem, Jerusalem, Jerusalem!' was all he could think of." The old man laughed heartily at his prayer. John told it on Dave for a joke and when Dave went down he began to laugh at him about his prayer. "You had better not wait until the devil comes again, Dave," and told us what John had told him. Dave said it completely hacked him out. That was funnier than ever. John would often tell jokes on Dave that way to hack him.

Brown just lived a short distance from our old home and Stevensons were on our place at this time. Gus had a trial and, for some reason, it was put off until the spring term, making bond for his appearance at the next term of court.

As Christmas was nearing, they began to talk about what they could do to pass off Christmas. Dave loved his dram and would always have whiskey about the place, if possible. I never approved of having whiskey about the place at all and would try to reason with him in regard to buying it.

"Oh, pshaw, I've always had my whiskey on Christmas and I'll have it this Christmas, too, if I live."

So, everything was planned. He would furnish the whiskey and they would have a high time. He had saved up money enough for all to get on a spree. It worried me no little. I knew he would get on a spree if no one else did. So, two days before Christmas, he saddled his horse, put on his spurs, and came to the door. "Where are you going, Dave?" I asked.

"I am going to San Saba today; be back tomorrow," he said.

I didn't know how much money he had or where it was. He jumped up on the bed and reached across and reached his hand into a hollow of one of the house logs. I was standing, looking at him.

"Diden," he said, as he drew his purse out, running his fingers through the purse at the same time and stretching it toward me, "the rats have eat up every doggone bit of the money."

I was so amused at his looks and actions. "How much did you have, Dave?" I asked.

"Fifteen dollars," he said.

I was dying to laugh. "Why did you put it there?"

"For safekeeping, of course," he said.

I burst into laughter. I couldn't help it.

"Yes, you would laugh if the world was coming to an end," he said.

He put it there when we went to leave the house in the flood and the rats had made themselves a fifteen dollar house. He couldn't find a number anywhere, so away went his Christmas money and his spree with it, and he lived until Christmas and didn't have his Christmas whiskey, either. We spent the Christmas so much nicer, I thought. No one was drunk and all had a jolly time.

Christmas evening we all went to the Browns. They were good old-timers and the old folks were members of the church. We sang religious hymns and cracked nuts and had, what I call, a splendid time. Numbers of people had moved in from Kentucky and all loved singing, which made a great improvement in society.

We had two roads from our house to Browns; one on the south side of the creek, which ran near our old home where Stevenson lived, and one on the north road. We mostly went the north road, unless we wanted to go by the store at Richland Springs. The store was kept by Captain Hayse, a fine old man; him being a witness against Gus, also.

We all went home after Christmas, everything passing on nicely, and on the eighth day of January, in the morning, Captain Hayse sent word to Jeff to come down. He wanted to see him on particular business. We guessed what he wanted in our mind. He drank hard and everyone thought every spree was his last. He was a great friend to us children and had no family of his own, and perhaps he aims to make a will to the children, was one decision. But Jeff, being just a boy, fourteen years old, wanted John to go with him.

"No," I said. "I don't want John to go. I am uneasy when he goes down there."

But Jeff continued to persuade him to go.

"Jeff, let him alone. He never does go prepared to defend himself and he is not going unprepared, and we have nothing here to shoot with," I said.

"Well, I'll borrow you a pistol if you will go," Jeff said.

"All right, then, go tell Frank Freeman I want to borrow his pistol."

When Jeff came, he said, "Frank said clean this pistol up; it won't fire. He dropped it in the creek."

"Oh, well, I won't need it anyway. I just got it to please Diden," John said.

"Yes, you will clean it, too," I said.

He was fixing his violin up. He got up and said, "Diden, I will give you my fiddle. You will have to get a treble string, though," and took the pistol and put it in his left side coat pocket, not even looking at it. Jeff had told him there were five cartridges in it and said, "Well, let's go now."

I begged him to see if it would fire.

"Oh, it is alright. I won't need it," he said, and walked off.

I had felt uneasy about him ever since I was told of his waylaying on the road, but I felt better this time, knowing he had a pistol. About an hour-and-a-half by sun that evening, I was sitting by the fire. It had been drizzling rain all day and Dave had stepped out. I called him and he came in. "Oh, Dave," I said.

"What is the matter with you," he said.

"Oh, John and Gus are going to kill each other," I said.

"Oh, what makes you talk that way? They won't," he said.

It passed by in a little while. I felt alright again. We live four miles from Richland Springs, just about three-quarters of an hour by sun. Dave and I were sitting by the fire and I heard three shots in quick succession. "Oh, Dave. There, John and Gus have killed each other."

"Oh, what in the world makes you have such spells?" he asked.

"Oh, I know they are dead."

He talked to me awhile and the spell passed again. I felt as usual until just after dark, and Jeff stepped in the door.

"Oh, John and Gus are both killed," I said.

"Yes," he said.

I never asked about the killing. "Where is John," I asked.

"At Riley's," he said.

We got on the animal Jeff rode and went. I rode behind Dave. When we got near enough to the house, I could hear John's groans. He wasn't dead, but fatally wounded. The bullet took effect just under the right nipple and came out under the left shoulder blade. The house was full of men and the doctor was there, doing everything possible, and him suffering agonies of death, and Gus lying a corpse just the other side of the road. Oh, what a touching scene for my nerves, but finding him alive gave me a great brace. Doctor Taylor said he had seen so many men get well, wounded as he was. That gave me great hopes of his recovery. Just after John went in and took his bed, John Stevenson came with a shotgun to kill him. The men objected to his admittance.

"Oh," he said, "I kept Gus from killing him last week as he was coming from Brown's. How I wish I had let him kill him now."

Brother John asked what he wanted and his friends told him. "Why, just turn my face toward the door and let him come," he said.

"No, no, it won't do. You have got your man and when his excitement is over, he will repent of his rash act," which was a fact. He was very sorry. Besides the fatal wound John received, he was shot through the right wrist, cutting all the leaders in two.

He wasn't expecting to be shot. Captain Hayse didn't get to put him on. Gus had kept his little brother in Hayse's store for a whole week watching for John to come in. Captain had kept a close watch on every maneuver and saw through the plot. He was convinced what the plot was when John came. Jimmy was to run home and tell Gus and he would kill John and the Captain, the main witnesses, and make his escape on his mother's fine animal he had got from her while the watch was kept. When John and Jeff stepped into the house, there was quite a crowd of customers in, trading, and Jimmy made his escape out and the Captain didn't see him. He was hurrying to get through to tell John what he thought the plot was and he wanted Jeff for that purpose, but John came, too. So, before he got through, Gus was there. John was sitting on a lounge, looking over a paper. Gus walked in and spoke and took a seat by him and talked awhile. Then he took hold of the paper and began looking over it, too, at the same time putting his arm around him.

After a bit he said, "John, I want to see you a moment. Step outside with me, please." They walked out and he asked John about a note he had got in possession of and thought John had wrote it, or claimed he did. The note made mention of him being a horse thief.

"No, I never wrote it. The shoe must fit you, or you wouldn't want to wear it," John said.

"Well, it is alright," said he, and turned to walk back, so John thought, but he wheeled back and threw his pistol down and fired. John, at the glimpse of the pistol, reached, or made an effort to reach, his pistol in his left side pocket. As Gus fired, shooting the leaders in two on his right hand at the wrist, the bullet penetrated his body.

John never staggered or fell, as Gus expected, and he wheeled and ran as John snapped his pistol at him, then fired, just as he turned the corner of the house; the bullet cutting through the corner. John went after him. He had squatted, as if trying to get under the house. When he saw John turn the corner, he ran to a fence that led from the other corner of the house and went to get over and just balanced on top of the fence. John said, "I took a bead aim and when my pistol fired, I knew I had him. God Almighty held him there. I don't claim I did it. I was too disabled to do anything if higher power had not assisted me. I was killed before I apprehended any danger." While he lay suffering, he could hear the distressing screams of Gus' mother coming to her lifeless boy and said, "Poor woman. I am so sorry, but I could not help it. I was murdered before I thought of perpetrating the act. It could not be helped."

He lived twenty-seven days after that. All during his suffering he said, "I don't feel I have committed any sin. I want to live to be baptized. That is a duty I put off until this trouble was over. I have been converted for some time and awaiting his trial, for fear I would be tempted to sin and could not live a faithful Christian. Now it is over. The first preacher I meet, I will demand baptism." He begged us to let him be buried with Christ in baptism, but we thought it would make against him and would not submit.

Oh, I was sorry we did not let him be baptized when I saw all hopes fading. He took hemorrhage of the lungs on the 26th of February and never rallied. At eleven o'clock the next day, the 27th of February 1878, his spirit took its flight and returned to God who gave it.

Chapter 14

Struggling Against the Wiles of the Devil

WHEN I SAW MY BROTHER laid out, a corpse, caused by the ministering angels of the devil, I could not shed a tear, but a great revenging spirit arose in my heart. Though an invalid, as I was, my heart swelled within me with such desperate thoughts. The note was carried to Gus by a widow lady's son. His mother and daughter said John had had it written by me and they could testify to my handwriting, when I knew nothing of it at all and was not at home at the time it was written.

I would try to pray. My prayers never went above my head. My heart only desired vengeance on those people. The inner man would say, "Quench not the Spirit but yield to Him now. In mercy He calls you. Come sinner and bow." I would try to reason in my soul but, oh, that horrid monster, the spirit of multitudes of demons would arise. I would find myself cutting their throats and the blood streaming, to my soul's delight, and when I came to know myself, I would be gritting my teeth and almost wild with terror. "Oh, my God, redeem my soul before it is everlastingly in the hands of these demons."

I can never remove from my mind my brother's calls, "Oh, Diden, do something for me, can't you? Oh, warm me."

"I will do everything I can, John." Mamma Brown and I

stood over him, wrapped warm blankets around him, but death's chilly hand was upon him.

"Oh, I am so cold, Diden. Poach me some eggs, quick, to give me strength."

I poached them and he ate them, but no strength came. To hear his dying pleas almost distracted me. I would try to remove my wretched thoughts, but I could not for a struggle of eight months, and a hard struggle, too. But thank God, by the help of the Lord, I regained my strength in the Lord.

I wrote to Jim, giving him all the particulars. He made arrangements and, the following November, he came home and brought a world of trouble to me. He had the same revenging spirit that almost bound me in chains to await my everlasting destruction. He had a reckless spirit, never saying but very little about it. I could now give him the proper advice. I was again myself. I lost no time in talking to him.

"Oh, my, I will have John Stevenson and Old Doc Gregg. They are mine. I'll teach old Doctor Gregg when he is called to a case to do all he can, not go off and say he would get well if a silver tube was inserted through the wounds, and not do it," Jim said.

John Stevenson left and Jim followed him, but Stevenson dodged him. Jim came back. I begged and pleaded with him to heed my words, but everywhere he went he would be told something that added to the fire already kindled. He went to Richland and came home and sat down by the fire. I was watching the expression on his face. He would turn pale as a corpse, then his face would flush a scarlet red. He reached in his pocket and brought out the bullet that John was killed with.

"Here is the bullet that John was killed with," he said.

Oh, I saw murder in his eyes. "Who gave you that bullet, Jim?" I asked.

"Doctor Taylor," he said. He jerked out his pistol, a cap and ball, and put the bullet in an empty chamber and capped it and ran to the door, wild with rage, and shot it in a tree. "Oh, if that were only Gus, I could feel better."

"Oh, Jim, don't talk so. John and Gus are both dead and it is God's will that that trouble be ended, and don't think anything you could do would better it. You can only bring on new trouble and destroy all your life and perhaps all the other boys' lives and mine. Now, try to be reconciled, for vengeance is Mine, saith the

Lord. Now try to look at this matter and take a reasonable view of the whole thing and you will feel better," I told him.

"Oh, I've got to kill those people. I can't rest. I'll kerosene that woman's house that sent the note and touch fire to it and burn the whole thing up," he said.

Here I used all my strength to remove this trouble.

He said, "Well, I'll tell you, I've got to leave here then. We can't all live in the same country."

"Jim, I don't want you to leave, but I would rather see you leave than to have you get into trouble," I said. I was at this time very poorly and had a severe cough, was seldom clear of fever, said to have consumption. I didn't think I could live through the rising of the sap.

Annie was now taking the young men's hearts. She was pretty and so modest and reserved. Jim was very proud of her, as well as myself. They spent the winter pleasantly together and when spring came, he went west. I passed over the spring with a rub and began to improve. Dave planted his corn and cultivated the ground once, after it came up. Oh, he had fine corn. It grew without scarcely any work at all.

As some of his friends said to him, "Dave, just plant your seed. That's all you have to do. It will make alright, while we work our crops and don't make any more than you do."

That summer Jim Hall bought a drove of cattle down east and Dave went to help drive them west. Before he left we made arrangements for Annie to go to school across on the San Saba River. He got a neighbor boy, a young man, to stay with Eli and me. Jeff was off at work, too. R. T. Roundtree was his name. He was in love with Annie and he gave me trouble about keeping her in school. He would go and bring her home without my consent. I finally told him what he must do. "You must remember Annie is not yours and there is nothing sure of her ever becoming yours. I want her in school and you make this your last time to bring her home, unless I send for her." The next Friday he had his brother to bring her home. I soon learned the whole family was working against me. Annie became disobedient, something surprising to me, and wouldn't go to school.

So, Dave came by, as he went with Jim's cattle, and we decided to let her remain at home, as she was so dissatisfied. She was then engaged to get married to R. T., but we didn't think of such a thing. The time was set; the fourth of July.

Dave went on with the cattle and located them on the Pecos River in West Texas where his brother, Jim, had started a ranch, and my brother, Jim, went to work on his ranch there. The Hall brothers had dissolved partnership in the ranch on the Cimmaron in New Mexico. So, Dave was gone a month.

When he came home, I told him Annie and R. T. were to get married soon and her only fourteen years old. He never opposed it; said R. T. was a fine young man. But when the time began to near, he proved untrue to her. I said, "Now, don't ever let him know you care the snap of your finger. It won't be very long until he will want your love again, and you deal with him falsely. Carry him as far as possible and drop him." She never lacked for suitors. She was very charming.

That fall we raised plenty of corn to do us. We had hogs aplenty for our meat, so we were doing fine, but Dave couldn't get over being beat out of his estate.

"I am going to see about that. I won't be robbed out of what my father and mother have worked for, beside all my labor, too," he said.

"Oh, let them alone. They'll pay you after awhile. I wouldn't have hard feelings among my brothers, if I were you," I said. I always felt that people would do unto me as I would do unto them. So, he said no more about it for some time. Finally, he consulted a party.

"Why, you can gain your part if you can make evidence to what your father had at his death."

He had the evidence but Oliver was still a minor heir. I didn't approve of him going to law. I thought they would at least give him a half loaf.

Things rocked on. We lived and got along alright, I thought, but I can't see how we did. All that winter I was very poorly, not able to be up very much of my time, and on March 22nd, 1879, my second child was born, a fine promising little girl called Amy, and she became the idol of our home. In July, the same year, Warren Hudson and Jim Hall moved back and resided near us; Jim being very rich. We had grown a small bunch of cattle and horses by this time. We had sold the sheep and Dave worked out with cattle. We had plenty of hogs in the woods. He kept them marked up. Occasionally, he would sell fat hogs but, still, doctor bills hung over him. Mid came back, too. He, of course, made his home with us. We went through the next winter all well. I partially regained my health.

The following summer, Mid got married and moved into the house with us. We never objected, of course, but we had taken his place for five years and we had only lived there two years and a half. Of course, I felt this was wrong of him, but he told Dave he could build on his land anywhere and he would let him have fifty acres of his land wherever he wanted to build. This was very trying on us, for we could only just live. We had no money to build with, so he went to work and cut and split post oak pickets and built a picket house. He made the boards to cover it with and made a chimney of mud and rock. Annie and I canvassed inside with white, worn out garments. We made it look snug inside but rough outside. We lived very comfortable in it, too.

That year was hard on us. It seemed we could hardly get along, but I got twenty milk cows from a man to milk, and we made a barrel of butter. Annie and I did all the milking ourselves. That brought us a little money, but nothing like we should of got, for we exposed ourselves the odd times in the rain. That winter, or fall, Dave and Mid borrowed $80 from Jim Hall and bought up a lot of hogs and took them to Llano to mast fatten them, but the mast was short and they didn't get very fat. So, I saved every eye of grease and made quite a chance of souse and sausage. I put up sausage for our own use and took the rest to San Saba to sell. I went as far as Aunt Nancy's and Dave and Uncle William said they would sell my sausage and lard and I need not go. So, on they went.

I still used my grass bed and pillows I made on Wilbargo. Aunt had a flock of geese and I did want a start of geese so bad, but never could have the money to buy any. When I thought they had had time to get back, I got restless. I knew Dave would get drunk and everytime he went to town, I was distressed until he came in. At night Uncle came in, and no Dave. "Where is Dave, Uncle?" I asked.

"Well, Diden, I sold your lard at twenty cents per pound. It brought you thirty-five dollars. I gave it to Dave and when I got ready to come out, he said he had lost it or said he put it in a box in the stove and couldn't find it," he said.

"He was drunk, wasn't he?"

"Yes, he was drinking, but not drunk," he said.

After night he came in. "Did you find your money, Dave?" Uncle asked.

"Yes, I found it," he said.

"Where did you find it?" he asked.

"In our empty tobacco box in the stove," he said.

Oh, I was sure proud. "I never sold all your sausage, Diden. I have a pan full left," he said.

Next morning he went out to the wagon and examined it and said, "This sausage is spoiled."

"Dave, let me look at it. It may just be old and not spoiled," Aunt said. She examined it. "Why it isn't spoiled. I will trade Diden out of it." So she came to the door. "I'll give you two geese and one gander for that sausage, Diden," she said.

"It is a trade now," I said. "Dave, you and Jeff go on the river and catch them." So, we got the geese and went home. I was well pleased with my little flock of geese.

Jim was still at Hall's ranch on the Pecos River and a young man about his age, named Jim Barbee, worked on an adjoining ranch and the two boys rode the same line and lived in a little house on the line together. They would ride all day on the line and come in at night and lodge in this little house.

It was a bitter, cold day, the 2nd day of January, 1880, and some freighters came up to the hut and took out and went in. No one was there, but someone is staying here, it is evident, so we will stay until they come. So, after awhile, the boys came in. The freighters were welcome. The boys went to cooking their supper, laughing and talking to each other. Jim Barbee began singing a foolish song.

Jim Harkey made the remark, "the one that composed that song was a fool."

Barbee continued to sing. All was fun, the freighters thought, as all were laughing.

Harkey said, "No one but a fool would sing that song."

Barbee set his frying pan down and went out to the corral and, in a few minutes, came to the door with his revolver in his hand and gave Brother the eye, and shot at the same time. Brother Jim was quick as a flash with his revolver. The freighters said they could hardly distinguish the shots apart. Barbee's took effect in Jim's bowels and Jim's first shot took effect in Barbee's heart; a dead shot. Jim shot him five times; each shot took effect in Barbee's body. The first shot Barbee received, he fell forward on his face. He only shot once, but made a fatal shot through Jim's bowels. When Jim saw he had killed him, he crossed his pistol over Barbee's on the floor and went and called to the men who had run out during the fight.

They asked if either one was hurt.

"Yes, we are both killed. I want you to go to the ranch after Dick Hudson, the foreman of the ranch, and tell him to come quick. I can't live but a few hours."

Jim saddled his horse, put one of the men on him, and directed him how to go.

"Now, don't lose no time."

It was fifteen miles to the ranch, thirty there and back. Dick got there before he died. He willed all his money and stock to Annie and Mose and Eli. He had just begun to accumulate property. He only lived a few minutes after Dick got there.

He said, "Oh, I wish Barbee had given me a dead shot like I did him."

This is all he said concerning their fight. All we knew about it was what the two freighters told.

He said, "Dick, I want you to see that Annie and Mose and Eli get what I have," and held out his hand to Dick. "Goodbye, Dick," he said in a whisper and gave his deathgrip goodbye.

Oh, how sad to think of my brother lying in that lonely little hut with his murderous rival, both corpses, way out on the lone prairies of Texas, not even a relative near him to speak a kind word of sympathy to soothe him in the agonies of death. Oh, if he had only been a child of God, then I could say in my heart, "Alone, yet not alone was he, though in that solitude so drear. For God has promised his children that he will never leave or forsake them." Now I had another burden of grief, but I understood better how to find rest for my weary soul. The Lord said, "Come unto Me, all yet that labor and are heavy laden, and I will give you rest. Take My yoke upon you and learn of Me, for I am meek and lowly in spirit and they shall find rest to your soul, for My yoke is easy and My burden is light." I knew he was the Lord's and in the hands of a merciful God and he would deal justly with him. There he was, away out there among his cowboy friends, one of the biggest-hearted boys in the world.

They dug a grave six by six and rolled each in a wagon sheet for shrouding and buried them just as they died. That was so hard to think of, but the boys could do no better. If they could, I am sure they would have put him away nice.

After the news went out in the papers, Barbee's father went to the ranch to learn the particulars. He said his son was there from disobedience. "He tried to kill me; stabbed me with this knife." He had a dirk knife the boys gave him of his son's in his hand. "He tried to kill me with a shotgun, but he is my boy and, as soon as I can, I shall remove his body home."

We knew Dick had done all that could be done then. So, we had to wait several months before we could remove Jim's body home.

When spring came, it was wet and warm and stock had shed off and were slick and fat by the 15th of March. Jim Hall was going to take a drove of cattle to his ranch and Champion had his gathered, too, to go with him. Now, I had to give up my cows, as they belonged to Champion. So, Dave and Jeff both hired out to Jim to make the trip. In a few days here came a blizzard, sleet, and snow, and everything hanging with icicles. When the weather moderated, all the vegetation looked like it was scalded. The grass had looked like a wheat field before the cold snap. Now everything lay flat on the ground. This delayed the drive west for some time.

I turned my attention to my little flock of geese I had traded my pan of sausage for that spring, and it was quite a task, too. In April, they started with the herd, leaving Annie and Eli and myself and little Amy at home. So, we got along fine. I had a fine bunch of gosling to see after, which was my delight. I could almost feel the soft feather beds I would have by next spring. I had one cotton mattress I had bought with my hogs and the rest were grass.

After they had been gone a week or so, we had one of the heaviest rains I ever saw fall and in a day or so one old horse came in for salt. I went out and salted him. I stood there looking at him. He was so fat and doing nothing. I walked up and caught him. "I'll just see if I can use you," I said. So, I led him up to the gate and tied him. "Annie," I said, "let's go over in Jim's field and plant some cotton to make us some mattresses."

"Alright. Eli, you bring the baby," she said.

So, over we went; never said a word to Jim's wife about it. We hitched him to the plow that set in the field. "Now, Annie, you drive and I'll hold the plow and we will lay off our rows." She started the horse. I tussled with the plow a few yards and it threw me down. I got up and tried it again but, in a few steps, down I came again and so on until I got to the end.

"Let me try it, Diden," said Annie.

"Alright," I said. So, she took my place and I drove; on a few steps and down she came. "It's Old Dick. The old rascal won't walk right," I said. Up she got and on we went, tussling and falling every few yards, until we got back to the end. Oh, I was so exhausted I could scarcely breathe.

"Eli, you try it awhile and Annie can rest and mind the baby," I said. So he took hold of the plow handles, with all confidence that he could man the plow, being only nine years old and without experience as well as we. I said "Now, hold the plow straight." I clucked to Old Dick and on we went, the horse fretting first to one side then to the other, Eli falling and getting up again, just as Annie and I had done, until he was exhausted. We exchanged places and continued to plow until we had something near an acre planted. It soon came up a fine stand.

Jim came over one morning, laughing, "Say, who has been farming over there in my field?"

"I, of course, Jim," I said.

"I'll tell you, Sallie, don't ever try to walk down one of those rows," he said.

"Why?" I asked.

"Why you will get lost. I never saw as crooked rows in my life," he said.

"Oh, well, there'll be more cotton grow in them than in a straight row," I said. Our rows were as crooked as any snake track I ever saw, but we raised our beds alright. We made three big, fat mattresses and all the quilt cotton we needed and had cotton left.

I raised nineteen goslings that spring and had two pet geese I had raised the previous year, and my three I traded for made me twenty-four head. I began to pick them as soon as the feathers got ripe. Every four geese would average one pound of feathers; made me six pounds at a picking and I picked every six weeks. I soon had fine feather pillows and feather beds and threw my grass beds in the wind I had used for nearly five years, renewing the grass occasionally.

While Dave was gone on his trip, he traded for a fine saddle animal and sent her in by Jim. I soon learned she was alright for me to ride. So, Annie had gone down in the neighborhood to spend a week with her friend and one of the Roundtree boys came by and wanted me to go over and see their new ranch home, situated near the Brady Creek at a large cave, from which they watered all their stock and for domestic use. I let Eli stay with Mid until I came back and I had the boy to saddle Dollie and I got on her and took Amy in my lap, and off we went. We soon made the trip of seven miles with all ease. Mrs. Roundtree was as glad to see me as if I were her daughter. Mr. Roundtree owned quite a large flock of sheep or a half-interest, rather. His partner was an Irishman, Mr. Gibbons, a bachelor who had come over from the old country recently; a character which will come into my life, a very rich man, later on.

He brought with him a friend, Mr. Bainsbridge, who had been very low with bone scurvy. For two months he lay off in a little side room all alone. I never saw anyone go near him, only Mrs. Roundtree when she carried him his meals.

"Mrs. Roundtree, doesn't anyone ever try to console him with cheerful words? I can't bear to know a living mortal, suffering as you say he does, is lying there and not go in to talk with him," I said.

I could feel in my heart his lonely suffering, away here in America without friends or relatives. Oh, my heart was full of sympathy for him. Mrs. Roundtree led me to the door, introduced me, and went about her duties.

He was lying with his head and shoulders propped up, writing poetry. "How are you, Mr. Bainsbridge? I've heard so many times of your afflictions and wished I could visit you and do something to relieve your pains," I said.

"Oh, no one can do that. If I could only get able to go home, I never would leave again. I never have written my mother my real condition. It would grieve her so, I keep it from her. I am so helpless, I lie here and write," he said.

He had sheet after sheet of paper scattered over his bed. I picked up a sheet, lying on a small table, and read it. It was a short poem. "Did you write this, Mr. Bainsbridge?" I asked.

"Yes, Ma'am," he said.

"Would you give this to me?" I asked.

"Ah, that is not good. I will write you a poem," he said.

He wrote a long poem for me on "The Wanderer." I have got it yet. He gained strength enough to start home and I have thought of that lonely stranger so often and wondered if he reached his native home beyond the deep, blue sea.

I stayed two days with my old neighbor, Mrs. Roundtree, and when I got ready to go, she said, "Here, Diden, look at my old cook stove. If you want it, you are welcome to it. I have a new one."

"Oh my, yes, and many thanks to you," I said. I went home rejoicing over my stove. I had cooked all my life over the fireplace and when Dave came home, I had a stove.

Four months after brother Jim was killed, we moved his body home and laid him by John's side in our home cemetery. This refreshed my grief and caused a gloom to come over me. We were pressed that year to live. Dave still thought over his estate, but I said, "Let it go if they don't give it to you. There is a way to get along." After reasoning with him over the matter, he dropped it.

"Well, I will go to work on our little place and improve it," he said.

"Now, Dave, get a deed to our land first, then what you do will be ours," I said. He went to see Mid to get a deed. He put him off just then. In a short time Mid sold the whole tract to Jim. Here we were, knocked out again. Jim let us remain in the house until he called for it.

Times began to oppress us. I never had worried about a living. I was in better health than I had been in for years, really since I was married, and my mind now ran on how we were to get along. Jim always seemed to think a great deal of me, really more than he did of Dave.

One morning he came over and after talking awhile, he said, "Dave, I came over to make you a proposition. You are in a hard shape and I would like to see you make something. I will let you have my carayard [sic] of horses to keep on the shares. You can brand me the third colt and you two-thirds, and you can breed your mares free to raise horses or mules, as you like, and I will give you $30 for every mule colt folded to your share and $15 for every horse colt folded to your share."

Dave never gave him any answer.

He said, "Now think it over and let me know," and went home.

"Oh, my gracious," I said, "don't let that chance slip. You take him up. If you can't make money out of that proposition, you can't make it out of anything." So, he went and took him up at his own proposal. He took possession of Jim's horses. We still lived in the picket house and Mid in the log house, until January.

Now, Annie had married. R. T. offered her his heart and she accepted it while she was engaged to another, but R. T. thought her true. He made preparations for housekeeping and one day he came in and told me that he and Annie was going to be my neighbor. They were going to get married soon.

"Are you?" I asked, very much surprised. A few days later he came back with a downcast expression. "Diden," he said, "I believe Annie is going to prove untrue to me. I have caught Warren Wood to see her several times."

"Well, R. T., I will tell you. She is to get married to Warren two days before she is to marry you. Now she has her revenge. I am the one that told her, when you proved untrue to her and almost broke her young heart, to cheer up. You would ask her love again and to carry you as far as possible and let you drop hard. Now, when you want to flirt again, don't flirt with an innocent orphan girl and take advantage of her youth, as you did Annie," I said.

The last of January 1882, we exchanged places with Mid. He moved in the picket house and we in the log house. It was a cold, wet February and Dave contracted a cold and it settled on his lungs, almost disabling him from business for several weeks, which worked a hardship on me, but my health had improved so much, I stood it wonderfully well. His cold left him with asthma, of which gave me no little trouble. In March, the 11th day, 1882, my third child was born, Essie May. An hour or two after her birth, I was left as dead. Yet at times my mind would return to me and I would hear a few words of the family grief over my supposed dead body and then I was gone again. Dave had sent for a doctor, but he hadn't yet come. Just as he stepped in the door, life returned again. I knew it was Doc Taylor's step and I was gone again.

"Dave, you are too late. She is dead," he said.

"Oh, please Doctor, try to do something," Dave said.

I never heard anything more for some time.

The doctor said, "I will try, but there is no use." He went to work, removed the cause of the hemorrhage and bound mustard poultices to my wrists and ankles and over my heart, and tried to get sweet milk in my stomach, the first thing he did, but it was quite a while before he succeeded. But when he did, it made new blood and finally he discovered there was yet life in me. After reaction set up, I began to cramp, yet I could speak. He, knowing the cause of my moans, set all about my bed to rubbing me. After so long, I spoke a whisper. "I am burning up."

"Take off the poultices, quick," he said and laughed. "Why didn't you send for me sooner?" But I didn't speak. After a while he said again, "Why didn't you send for me sooner?"

"Doctor, — it — was — all — I could — do to — say — go — when — I — did," I said. I had been swooning from the very birth of my child, but no one knew it. I would think, "I'll tell Dave to send for Taylor," but then I was gone in a swoon. That was on my mind. When I came to, I was so weak and, in an instant, I was gone. At last I said, "Go after Taylor," and my demand excited them all. He was brought as quickly as possible. It was a very dark night and Oliver, Dave's brother, started in great speed and his animal stumbled over a plow and fell with him. Fortunately, neither one was hurt and the animal never ran as she normally did. He lost no time in bringing the doctor, for his animal was fleet of foot. The doctor stayed until late the next evening.

"Now, if you are particular, you will get up, but your recovery demands the best of care," he said.

Now Dave had experienced the loss of me and being left with those little babes to care for; not really what it would have been, but a mere foretaste, put a different feeling in his heart for me. He became very kind to me and nursed me through with the help of relations. He became more careful with me. We remained in the log house all that year. I got able to work, but never saw a well day.

Mose had come to us during this time and Jeff had gone west to work on Jim's ranch. We were doing fairly well. Dave got the cash down for his part of the colts, which amounted to a nice little sum. That fall he took me down to his sister's, as he often did, to stay a couple of days and left Mose at home to water and feed the jack and stable horse. The weather was very threatening when we left so, that night, Mose got up and when he threw his feet off the bed, they were in water. The little fellow was scared almost to death. Finally, he decided to make it to a pecan tree near the house. He made it alright and climbed it and sat there until the water subsided from the house. When we got home, everything in the house was ruined. Such a mess I never saw before, but we cleaned and scraped and saved what we could, which was very little; the water being over two feet deep in the house. The next spring we moved back to the picket house.

During this time, we had bought a section of land on the head of the Wilbargo. I had a time to get him to buy it. After he had bought it, he said he had no use for so much land and wanted to sell half of it at the price he paid, $1 per acre. Oh, I did beg and tried to show him what the future would bring when land would advance to a high price.

"Oh, pshaw, there will be land lying out as long as I live," he said.

We were just opposite in our ideas. He looked only at the present time and I looked at the future and present. He kept after Mid to take half of it. He thought, too, there would always be plenty of land for all stock, but at last he took half of it, to my sorrow. I wanted it, so he was relieved and I was grieved.

Jim always liked me, seemingly, better than he did Dave. He always loaned me his carriage when I wanted to make a trip. During this time, Joe had been elected sheriff of the county and his wife and three children were spending a few weeks with me, and Jim sent us his carriage to use while she was there. We had made a date to spend the day with Mrs. Jim Richard and, as I was detained with a new hive of bees to see after, we were late, so I said, "We will have to drive to get our name in the pot, giving the horses a keen cut at the same time." As I did, one of the lines slipped out of my hand and, knowing one of my horses was not safe, it excited me and I raised up and began to "So, Ho, Ho," pulling the one line.

Henrietta said, "Don't pull the line. You will turn the carriage over."

I saw then what I was doing, in my excitement, and thought to sit down. I went to the ground, for the seat was not where I expected it to be and, of course, holding the one line, I jerked the horses around so they upset the carriage with five children and

Henrietta closed in. It was a closed carriage. I jumped in front of the horses and stopped them. In a few minutes, there were two ladies came to us and helped the children out; only two being hurt: Sam Harkey and Sallie, my brothers' children. The blood was streaming. I was excited out of my wits. They sent for a surgeon and had the gashes stitched up, which took several stitches, and they will wear the scars to their graves. One was across Sallie's forehead and one across Sam's cheek. We set the carriage up. Two of the wheels were badly dished.

When I got over my excitement, Taylor said, "I thought you had quite a little sense, but this don't look like it," laughing.

"It certainly doesn't, I admit," I said. We went home from there and didn't drive anymore. That was enough for us both.

Jim laughed at me about being an expert driver but, knowing I was weak and nervous, he made me feel better by saying, "Well, Sallie, you need not worry about my carriage wheels. I feel proud that no one was killed. I think you were all very fortunate. I can soon have the wheels fixed and you can use it when you want it again."

He was so kind to us; always a friend in need and not only to me, but every poor person. He was a poor man's friend. He knew my parents long before I was born. My father was a friend to him when he first started out in the world.

Chapter 15

Hot Springs, Haunts, and Half-wits

OUR FUTURE PROSPECTS KEPT me up and doing all I could, yet I was very despondent, being alone with the children so much. Dave was out on the range all the time and when night came, I could only sit and think, "Why doesn't he come home? I know he can't do anything after night and I know the horses are all corralled and everything fed long ago." My first dread was he may have gotten whiskey some way and is tight. Oh, mercy, if he would only come home and be punctual with me. I never knew what to depend on. Then my heart would swell in grief and my mind wander off in agonies of grief for my murdered brothers. "Oh, how can I ever bear so much; all my family so scattered with only two little brothers," I thought.

I soon had all my troubles collected together in a head and would sit and cry and long for Dave to come home until late in the night. Then I would look to my Lord in sincere thanks and supplication to lift my burdens and help me to bear my troubles, then lie down with relief but not to sleep until Dave came. I would lie and listen to hear the sound of his horse's hoofs, which sometimes would reach the hour of eleven, and when he would come, I would say, "Dave, what have you been doing? I have been so uneasy."

"Ah, that's all I can hear. I am able to take care of myself. You needn't be bothering about me," he said.

"Well, where have you been?"

"I've been at Jim's [Dave's brother] or Warren's," he would say.

When he came, I felt happy even if he didn't ever talk to me, but when he had to go to town, I was distressed. No one knew but me. I knew he would take too much whiskey and if he had any money, he would sure lose it some way, but he never gambled it off, for he never indulged in any kind of games. He would carelessly lose it out of his pockets or stick it away somewhere and never know what he had done with it. The odd times I have sent Mose to see after him when he was late getting in. I knew it would make him mad, but I would be so uneasy, I couldn't help it.

I never did get vexed at his cross words, for I was so glad to see him come. His harsh words would pierce my heart for an instant and they were forgotten. I held such a deep love for my family, I could forgive most any act or words. I always was very kind to him when he returned home drunk. I cared for him just as tenderly as if he was sick physically, but so sorry to think he would drink so, when my desire was to rear a perfect family. When he would get sober, he would feel ashamed of his conduct. Then I would reason with him in kind words and show him how little he respected me and how little he regarded my love. He never disputed a word of my advice, but admitted I was right and he was a brute.

That fall most everybody was sick; hardly enough well to wait on the sick. Jim's wife took down and Jim couldn't get anyone to help nurse her. I went and stayed a few days and went back and forth, doing my own work, until she became so low I couldn't leave her. Then I remained with her all the time. The doctor told me if I didn't drink whiskey, I would certainly break down, "For," said he, "you have no strength anyway. I can't see how you bear up like you have for twelve days; two babies to care for and Jim's wife, too." Essie was now seven months old and Jim and Marie's baby three weeks old and I was yet weak and very thin in flesh, but I had an iron will that never faltered as long as I could do any good. Jim, at last, got a girl to come and stay. Willie Allwine was her name, and that relieved me, but Mary was convalescent before I left her.

My health continued poorly all winter and when spring

came, I grew worse. Yet, I did my house duties by keeping a woman to do my washing; a very poor woman whose husband was in the state penitentiary and had to work to support herself and four children. I paid her a dollar every day she worked. Besides, I would give her pork and the odd pound of bacon. I never can see anyone in distress. If it is possible to help them, I certainly will. My childhood circumstances presents it real to me. I think of the many times I have passed Brown's going to school with an empty stomach and, my hunger so great, I could have reached my hand in to Mamma Brown's slop pail and partook of the scraps of sweet potatoes and relished them. But I can conscientiously say there never was a drop of dishonest blood ran through my veins. I was too high-minded to do a thing so low as that or ever insinuate I thought of doing such. The poor lady's husband was finally reprieved and I rejoiced in my heart for her when she was released from the washtub.

Now, Jim's wife was in wretched health and Jim began to arrange his business to move to California for her health and go by way of Hot Springs, Arkansas, and stop over there several weeks and try the waters there. He wanted me to go as far as the Springs with them. He said it would cure me, as I was subject to rheumatism, and they were highly recommended for that, but I objected. I felt differently about it being a benefit to me but he made Dave and Joe think it would cure me and they insisted on me going until I, at last, gave my consent to go. I never wanted to, as I felt it would make against me, but I made ready to go and, when the time arrived, I packed my trunk and, leaving little Amy behind with her Aunt Susan, I took my baby, Essie, seventeen months old, and drove to San Saba and stopped overnight with Joe. I told Dave and Joe, that night, I didn't want to go, but they wouldn't hear to me not going.

So, the next morning the stage drove up early. Oh, I did shriek at the idea, but they would have me go. I said no more, but bid them good-bye and took the stage for Lampasas that day. When we arrived there, I was very much fatigued, for it took the entire day with hard driving to make the trip and the road was dusty and hot and dry. We got there just before sundown. We washed and dressed for supper. In a few minutes, we took supper and then prepared to retire until train time the next morning at three. I didn't rest scarcely any, nor little Essie, either. We were both too much worried from our drive to rest but at half past two the next morning the doorbell rang to get ready for train time. We were ready and, by train, we got in to Fort Worth at three that evening and laid over until four the next morning. Little Essie took sick that night, but nothing serious. The water affected her bowels. We had a three days and nights run from Fort Worth to Hot Springs. We got in there at four o'clock in the morning, all worn out for sleep. We took a sleeper, but we never slept much.

We put up at Mrs. Davis' hotel when we first went in and all the hotel proprietors were drumming for certain doctors and the doctors drumming for hotels. So, Mrs. Davis caught Jim as a patron for Doctor Adams. "Oh, he is the finest doctor here. Don't fail to consult him." Jim wasn't long about consulting him, so he advised Jim to take lodging for Mary and I in the suburbs of town at a nice little cottage where it was more healthful. So, the old lady escorted us out and showed us the rooms, very nicely furnished, and our meals brought to us for $10 a week. So, Jim rented two rooms; one for me and one for his wife and children, Marie's being better furnished than mine, but she was to furnish mine later on. Next thing was to get a doctor to diagnose our case, so Doctor Adams was the only doctor. Jim hired him to treat Mary and I for $100 a month, $50 each, the cash down in advance. He was to visit us every day and give directions for baths and treat our children, should they need a physician. Next was to make arrangements for our baths. He made a deal at the Ozark Bath House. I bought $5 worth of tickets for each of us at the Ozark Bath House. My bathroom number was 5. After he made the necessary arrangements for us, he returned back to Texas on a business trip.

So, the next morning we went down in the city to take our bath and take a bird's eye view of the situation of the town. To hear the people that resided there speak of their city, you would think it was situated in a valley but, instead, it was located along the spring branch, which made its way down through very high, rough mountains; the foundations of the most magnificent, three and four stories high, were dug down to a level with the bank, which made the street along the branch on each side. The whole town was set in those rough mountains. To just drive along and look straight ahead, it is a beautiful town, but turn your eyes to either side and see the rugged mountains, where you could step off of the top of most any building on to the mountain, it made me feel like the earth was closing in on me. I didn't like the situation at all. The inhabitants were so hard-hearted, they all seemed to be void of sympathy toward humanity. Of all the suffering and misery there was to be seen there, all kinds of diseases and cripples, no one ever took notice of the other. If you got in distress and needed help, you got it if you had a full purse. If not, you did the best you could without help.

Essie continued to grow worse and in a few days was very ill. I only took two baths until I was aware that I couldn't bear them. The third morning the doctor gave me instructions; ten minutes warm bath and one minute vapor bath. I gave my instructions to the superintendent, an old Negro woman.

"Alright, Honey," she said.

She put me in a warm bath and kept me there ten minutes, then out and into the vapor for one minute. She closed me in and shut me up and went on to another patient. I couldn't see light at all. In a few seconds, my head seemed dizzy. I called to her, but no response. Then my head would seem to whirl again. I called Puss again, but still no response came. I began to try to get out. I clawed and pulled and lifted at the yoke over my neck. At last I got fresh air and kept clawing and pushing until I got out. I was about out of the scrape. I couldn't stand up. I waited a few seconds to regain my strength and returned to my room and was trying to dress when old Puss came running in.

"Lord de, Massy, Honey, how did you ever get out by yourself?" she asked.

"Why did you go off like that and leave me in that trap? I came very near not getting out," I said.

"Oh, mercy, that was too much for you. You can't take the vapor bath," she said.

"Oh, yes, I know I can't without you telling me now," I said. That was my last bath. I got back to my room feeling very poorly and Essie to care for, too, may be more than I can stand. I knew my baby would die and I never thought of my pains. I was only thinking of her and how I would take her corpse home. During this time Doc Adams was killed for his rascality and Jim's wife took very ill the next night after his return from Texas and he called in Doctor Collins. After he prescribed for her, Jim sent him to my room to see me, but I was not in need of him for myself, but my baby. "Doctor, can't you do something for her?" I asked.

"Very well," he said and got up and went to Jim's room. "Mr. Hall, you go down in town with me. Your sister is in a very dangerous condition. She is liable to drop off at any minute."

So, after a bit, Jim came in with a load of medicine for me to take. "Oh my, Jim, didn't he send any medicine for my baby?" I asked.

"You take this medicine now. He said you needed it and your baby wasn't very sick," he said.

I began to take it. At dinner the doctor came.

"How are you feeling?" he asked.

"Oh, I'm alright, but my baby is very sick," I said.

"Oh well, she'll be alright soon," he said.

At night he came again and never noticed my child either time. The next morning he came.

"How do you feel this morning?" he asked.

"Well, I am sick this morning, Doctor," I said.

He took my temperature and said, "I have the disease under control now."

I thought I was very sick, which I was, but had just become conscious of my suffering. I lay three weeks before I got up. I hired a girl to wait on me and the baby. Jim insisted on sending a telegram to Dave, but I objected. I told him I guessed I would get able to go home soon and I would, just as soon as I was able to get out of my bed. So I did the third day after I got out. I told Jim I was going home.

"Oh, you can't stand the trip yet," he said.

"Oh my, I can't stay here. I've got to try to get home with my baby. We will both die if I stay another month," I said. So, he took us to the depot and saw me off. I had a hard trip but, by the help of new friends, I made it through to San Saba to my brother's in a worse condition than when I left. I was gone seven weeks and when I came back, I was using crutches to walk with and had dropsy of the bowels. Joe sent me home in a few days. I stayed at home three weeks and Dave took me back to San Saba and put me under Doctor Gregg's treatment for six months. During this time, Dave moved from the picket house, three miles west on the Plant and Bacon Ranch, which Jim now owned; it being a better location for a home ranch than where we lived. I lingered along. Sometimes hope was almost gone for my recovery, but near Christmas Dave moved me home.

He had a family in the house with him, which proved a help to me. They were very kind people and the lady cared for my little girls as though they were hers. The house was situated on the south side of Richland Creek. It was a beautiful place with mesquites in the front yard that had been pruned for shade trees, and a heavy grove of pecan timber on the creek just north of the house. Just beyond was a beautiful little farm we had to our own use. The house was much better than I was used to; it having four rooms and out houses. In a few months, I began to improve slowly. The Cochran family remained with us until March.

Just a few days before they moved out, she said to me, "Mrs. Hall, this house is haunted."

I looked at her in astonishment, for she was above the average woman for intelligence. "Why, Mrs. Cochran, I thought you were more intelligent than to think of such folly as that. Don't you know there aren't such things?"

She laughed. "Well, I never thought there was until I moved here, and I won't argue with you about it but, when you hear it, you will think different."

"Oh, pshaw, it is wood rats," I said.

"Alright. You will think different after awhile," she said.

The place was settled by two foreigners when I was only a lass and the public road ran just south a little distance, and it was quite a distance to Brady City and eight miles to Richland; just a lone ranch way off there.

After awhile she said, "I tell you when you hear it, it will strike three hard strikes, as with a hatchet against the wall, in quick succession and stop." So that ended the haunt story just then and I thought no more about it.

About three weeks after they were gone, about ten o'clock one night, I was lying awake meditating when, all at once, bang! bang! bang!, like one striking the walls with an ax. It sounded like a cannon to me. Oh my, my hair stood on end. I lay still, my heart in my mouth. At last I reached over and shook Dave and whispered, "Are you awake, Dave? Did you hear that?"

"Yes," he said in a whisper.

Neither one of us spoke another word that night. The next morning we discussed the haunt question. Neither of us believed in haunts, yet it was an evident fact that wood rats could not strike with such force as those knocks produced. We never spoke to anyone about the mysterious sounds. I didn't want anyone to think I was superstitious. "So, I'll never say anything about it," I thought. In a short time we heard it again. "Dave, that's someone striking against the pantry room. Get the lamp and let's see," I said. The house was built north and south with a side room on the west and a partition which was used for a bedroom on the south end and a pantry on the north. The knocks were always in the north end of the side room and pantry. So, we made a search, but found no one.

"It can't be anybody, for there is no one lives near us but Old Man Smith and I know it isn't him," I said.

"No, he can't see well enough to be out at night."

The first visit Mrs. Cochran made us she asked, "Well, have you heard the haunt?"

"Well now, we've heard the haunt and it doesn't get old, either. It sets my hair straight on my head everytime it knocks. We can't find anything about the place, yet it sounds just like someone with an ax or heavy hatchet and strikes in quick succession, three hard licks."

"Well, I told you this place was haunted. We hunted for someone, too, but never found anyone. I was told by Mrs. Plant that it worried them all the time they lived here," she said.

I often had to be alone and when Dave had to be away, he would get Miss Mattie Cochran to stay with me. He was going to make a horse hunt up in Coleman County and she came down on Saturday. He was going away on Monday and he had a bunch of hogs he was keeping close around, going out every evening and driving them in. So, Saturday night he was out after his hogs and Mattie was sitting in front of the door sewing.

"Mrs. Hall," she said, "I wish that haunt would come tonight. I would sure ask it what it wanted. I wouldn't do like you and Mama."

"Well, I would like to know what it wanted, but its disturbance is so quick I can't rally my brains in time to think what to say," I said. The moon was shining bright and Dave had not yet got within hearing with the hogs. She was very busy with her sewing and I was listening, as usual, for Dave. I was sitting, looking out the door, when, seemingly, a man stepped on the porch with a pair of spurs on his feet, apparently walking about on the porch. I could hear him, but couldn't see anyone, while I stared with all my eyes. Oh my, I almost sank. I thought of what Mattie had said about asking the haunt what it wanted and here it was to relate its mystery. It was several seconds before I could speak. At last I said, "Mattie, why didn't you ask it what it wanted?"

"Why, that was Mr. Hall," she said.

"No, it wasn't. I've been sitting here trying to see someone but there wasn't anybody near," I said.

"Oh, that was Mr. Hall. I heard his spurs rattling," she said.

"Well, I heard the spurs but it was not Dave. Don't you know the dogs are not here and he unsaddles here at the porch and we can't hear the hog bell? Now let's go out and see," I said. So, we went out and looked all about the house but saw no one. We kept very quiet and kept a keen ear for the hog bell. In the course of an hour, we heard him at quite a distance, coming. The hogs had got quite a long distance from home and made him late. Then she was convinced it must have been the haunt but it never had come in that way before or since.

That fall Jim [Hall] came back on business and came out to see us. At the supper table I asked him if he believed there was such a thing as a haunt.

"No," he said.

"Well, I never did either, it sounds so suspicious, but let me tell you, I have changed my mind. This place is haunted without a doubt," I said. I related the story to him.

"Well, Sallie, I would not doubt what you say but I expect someone is trying to scare you," he said.

"Well, Jim, they have tried to scare everyone that has occupied this house then," I said.

"Well, I thought I would give you this house but I don't suppose you would have it if it is haunted," he said.

"No, indeed. If I have to live in it, I don't want it. I know I never have done anything to be haunted. It won't harm me, I am sure, but I don't like to hear anything about the place and can't account for it," I said.

"Well, I'll give the house to you and you can have it moved on your land. I don't guess it will follow the house," he said.

We remained on the place two years.

We had bee hives all around the house, which kept me busy all through the spring season hiving young swarms of bees and seeing after my flock of geese and caring for my two little girls. I had gotten from under the doctor for awhile. I had sold a number of pounds of feathers at seventy-five cents per pound and that year we took honey from the hives and filled everything, from small buckets to ten-gallon cans and one forty-gallon barrel, with honey. Dave was always out until late at night; just my two little girls and myself alone all day long until the horse herd came in at night. I never apprehended any danger in the least, and living near the public road, too, until a fright I had one day.

I was washing and had my wash tub on the north side of the dining room and the two little girls were in the dining room playing. I was busy rubbing, with my head down, and an uneasy feeling came over me, one of approaching danger. I instantly raised and turned around and there was a man within two feet of me, slipping up. I stepped in the door and then spoke to him and told him to walk around to the porch. He stood there looking about the place. "Go around to the porch, Sir," I said, "and have a seat." Then he turned and went around. I walked in through the dining room and into the front room and picked up my shotgun and walked to the door. Sitting in just by the door, he never saw my gun. I stood in the door to hear what he wanted. He began to ask how near was my nearest neighbor and who lived in a tent just beyond the field and then asked if my husband was about the home. I reached my gun, holding my hand on it. "Sir, what is your business here? I have given you time to tell your business," I said. I lifted my gun up in my hand. "Now it is time for you to travel, as you have told your business." He took me at my word and was not long in getting off. After that, I kept a watch when I was alone.

We had accumulated, by this time, quite a good start and I never thought of hard times now. Dave always provided well for his house. He rented the farm out, as his time was occupied with his stock. The third year the creek overflowed the farm and almost ruined the crop, yet we raised considerable oats and wheat. We had plenty of hogs, as it was a fine hog country. All he had to do was to take his hog dogs and go out in the woods and drive them in and kill them, no expense whatsoever. I never thought of being out of nice fat hams and all the lard and meat we possibly could use and all the honey and butter and sausage and anything I wanted and Dave making money all the while.

Yet his little sprees were so humiliating to me. If he would only leave that off, I would be happy. When he started to town, I

was in distress until he came home. Yet, he never was unkind to
me when he came home intoxicated but that base habit I ab-
horred so much. I felt I could never arise to the elevation my soul
so anxiously desired. I would look at my two little girls; two perfect beauties they were. "Will my two little angels be brought low
and abased by a drunken father? God forbid that such a disgrace
come upon them." This was my trouble now. My brothers were
all able to make their living, yet my soul reached out after them
on the distant plains. If only Dave would heed my pleading to not
drink anymore, I would feel a free, happy woman and my soul
ready to take its flight to the realms of unknown bliss.

That fall he had to attend court and he contracted measles. I
never had had them and the doctor told him if I took them I
never would get up, my health was so poorly, and we believed it,
of course. He took down. In time my little girls both took them. I
nursed them all until they were able to sit up and then I took
down but, with a hard rub of three weeks, I began to improve. All
that winter I was very poorly, but did my work and cared for my
little girls.

The next spring we rented the farm to a family of half-witted
people, very poor people they were, and I felt so sorry for them.
I would give them milk and butter and I had a nice turnip patch
of which I gave them free access. When spring came I had my
garden put out and I attended it with a hoe, besides my young
goslings to care for of which I had a large bunch. I had, by now,
got very tired of the haunt and I persuaded Dave to move on our
land. So, he began to make preparations to move after the crops
were made and the horse work was over. He hired help and, at
intervals, improved our new home. When my garden vegetables
came in, I was liberal with my neighbors to divide all varieties of
vegetables. I had found that the children would filch, but I felt
that it was caused by hunger and when I would catch them with
anything, I always called to them and talked to them. "Now, children, when you want anything I have, just tell me. I will give it to
you. Don't take any in this way. This is stealing and don't ever
steal from me, for you can get it by asking for it." My garden was
some distance from the house and it was wearisome to me to go
after my vegetables after I had done my chores of mornings. I
had gone several mornings and failed to get any tomatoes. This
worried me worse than my walk, for I was satisfied in my mind

the Arnells were stealing them. They were bothering me already by killing my geese and had killed a fine sow and left a nice litter of fine pigs that died. So, I went to see the old lady. "Mrs. Arnell, I want to talk to you in regard to your boys killing my geese. They have killed several and I wish you would please have them let them alone. You don't know how hard I have worked to raise them. I don't believe you would approve of your children damaging me and, if you will have them leave the tomatoes alone, there will be tomatoes for us both."

"Now, Mrs. Hall," she said, "my boys don't kill your geese nor bother your tomatoes."

I said no more to her, for I was sure in my mind then that she knew all about it and was harboring her boys in their deeds. I went home vexed. I went the next morning, as usual, to the garden and picked out some of the nicest tomatoes I could find and the ones that would ripen first. "Now, how can I catch the one that is doing this stealing? I don't want to injure anyone nor won't." I thought over the matter all the way to the house and finally it came to me how I could catch the thief and not kill them or injure them physically. I went in to my medicine box and brought out a vial of Ipecac. I took my penknife and vial of Ipecac and turned back and walked with delight, thinking, "Now I will catch the old lady and her daughter." So, I took my knife and split the tomatoes just at the stem and put what I thought a full dose to make them sick enough to report it, whoever got the dose, and went back to the house laughing in my sleeve. I thought the tomatoes would be ripe enough to pull by next morning. I never told anyone what I had done, but thought over it quite a great deal that night. I didn't know whether I was acting as a Christian or not, but I knew it would only make them sick and perhaps break them from stealing. I finally got my conscience satisfied and went to sleep.

I rose early next morning, hurried with my work, and put out to my garden, the two little girls following behind me. I got to the garden and walked, very unconcerned, down the tomato rows. I glanced at my baits and saw they were just turning; the little girls still following behind me. They found my baits and, of course, like all little ones, pulled them. I thought, "What if those children find my baits and eat them," and, turning, they had them just ready to take a bite. "Children," I hollered, "don't you eat that. Throw them down! They are not ripe enough." I took the tomatoes and threw them away. "Now I've got to put out another bait. I won't be out done. I know I'll catch my thief." I went back to the house and got my knife and medicine and put out a new bait. I gave them plenty of time to ripen before I went back. When I went, my baits were all gone. "Now, I'll just keep my ears open. I know they have stolen them." The next week following, Mrs. Powell, living north of them, came over to visit me.

She had not visited very long until she said, "Mrs. Hall, did you know Mrs. Arnell and Mary, her daughter, almost like to have died a few days back?"

"Why, no, what was their ailment, Mrs. Powell? I never heard. Do you know how they were taken sick, Mrs. Powell?" I asked.

"Why, yes, they took to vomiting," she said.

"Do you know how they are now?" I asked.

"Yes, they are all up now," she said.

"How long were they sick?" I asked.

"I think all day and night," she said.

"Well, I hadn't heard it. I am glad they are alright again," I said.

"Yes, I am too, the poor things. They are to be pitied," said Mrs. Powell and we dropped the subject.

When Dave came in that night, I said, "Dave, I have caught the thief that has been stealing my tomatoes."

"How? Who was it?" he asked.

"It was the old lady and Mary; just who I told you it was," I said.

"How did you find out it was them? I don't believe they have been stealing them," he said.

"You can't guess how I found it out, but I know it was them now," I said. I never had done a mean deed in my life and I didn't feel like I had done a very bad trick now, but I knew he would be surprised at what I had done. I then told him.

"Well, I'll say. Did you do that? What if you had killed them?" he asked.

"Oh, I didn't aim to kill them. I didn't bait to kill. I baited to catch and I caught, too. Now they'll leave my tomatoes alone so that I can get a few messes;" and they did, too. I wasn't troubled about my garden anymore, but the vegetable time was nearly over then.

Chapter 16

At Home in Deep Distress

THE HORSE WORK WAS now over and we were making ready to move on to our new home. Our land was located in a dry region; no water courses near it. We had to make surface tanks for water, which required some time. This gave me considerable worry, for I had my flock of geese and they required water. I studied over it quite a little. I had made money selling feathers and had all the nice beds and pillows I needed, but I wanted to hold them and see what my pan of sausage would bring me, and now I would have to dispose of them. I only had twenty-seven head left. The Arnells had killed nearly half of them So, I thought, "Maybe I can trade my flock for something that will increase." So, in a few days, Mrs. Powell came over and wanted my flock and they had a flock of goats they wanted to sell. "Mrs. Powell, how would you like to trade your goats for my geese?" I asked.

"That will just suit me," she said.

"How many have you, Mrs. Powell?"

"I think there is eighty head, all young, too," she said.

"Well, I will trade you head for head, but I only have twenty-seven head now, but will take all you have and pay the difference in money."

"It's a trade now," she said.

My sausage had increased considerably. The goats were on

121

Deep Creek, about seven miles from where we were going to move. So, I delivered the geese and Dave was to go after the goats, but he put it off from time to time, and I never did get him to go until the wolves had devoured my whole flock. This grieved me, for I had worked so hard for four years and now I had lost it all but my money I had got for my feathers, and my beds and pillows.

So, in August, Dave began to move my haunted house. I told him, if there had been a murder perpetrated in the house, maybe the haunt would remain where the body was buried and not follow the house, for I had it in my head that some traveler had been knocked in the head with an ax and murdered in the room where the licks always were heard at ten or eleven o'clock at night, except when the traveler walked over the porch when Miss Mattie wanted it to come to ask it what it wanted. The day before we moved the last room, I was sitting, sewing near the center of the front room about one o'clock in the afternoon and our horse-herder was sitting in the door and "whack, whack, whack" against the walls of the house, just where it had always struck. Never hearing it in the daytime, I thought someone was hammering on the wall. I got up and called the little girls. They were off some distance from the house. I went out and looked for somebody, but found no one. I came back and sat down. I knew it was the haunt.

"Who was that knocking against the house?" the boy asked.

"No one," I said.

"Why, I know it was," said Blackwell. "It almost shook the bottles off the mantelpiece."

"It is a haunt, Blackwell. You didn't know this place was haunted, did you? I never like to tell such yarns, for I know people won't believe it. I know what I thought of anyone that told such things, while I know this is a fact, but I would rather people would find it out just like I have and be convinced," I said.

I believed someone was buried under the floor so strong, I had them to dig for the body when they moved the room. When anyone was there and heard it, then I would tell them all about it, but I knew it was hard to believe and I didn't want anyone to doubt my word on anything, is why I didn't like to tell it. So, we moved our house and left the haunt. It never bothered us anymore. I wouldn't go camp over that old house place today. I heard it all I cared to, is why.

We moved when we did and Dave turned the horses back to

Jim and we started out on our own hook to improve our new home. We had, by this time, a nice bunch of cattle and horses. We fenced a small pasture first, then I wanted a farm but he didn't. He said we had no use for a farm, but I never rested until he cleared some ground, or had it done, rather, and fenced it.

That fall we got a family to take care of our home and we moved to Richland to be near a doctor, as I was very decrepit all summer, and the 22nd of October 1885, another son was born to us. James Mathias, we called him. I was in dread all the time we were there, for there was plenty of whiskey there, but [Dave] never got intoxicated the whole two months we were there.

When our little boy was one-month-old, we moved home again. I was very delicate, not able to take care of myself and baby. Dave did the housework and took care of the children and me. In a few days, after our return home, he said he was going to Richland one morning. "What do you want to go for, Dave?" I asked.

"Well, I want to go, and I am going," he said.

"You will come back this evening, won't you?"

"Yes," he said.

So, off he went. It was very cold weather and he carried in wood and built a good fire in the fireplace and piled up wood by the side of the fireplace to keep me a fire all day, and he had plenty cooked in the kitchen. We fared very well, but my spirit was troubled all day. When night came, I became more distressed yet. I couldn't believe he would get drunk, as we had been near the parson two months and he never drank a drop. Dark came and I put my last piece of wood on the fire to have a good fire when he came, for I knew he would be very cold, riding horseback fifteen miles in the bitter, cold night air. I waited and listened. "Oh, why doesn't he come? Here I am alone, not able to put the children to bed and the little things are so sleepy and the fire will soon be out."

I sat and cried and thought, "Oh, what an unfortunate girl I have been. Oh, if Mother could only have lived to comfort my broken heart here alone and no one to love and care for me in my weakness and afflictions."

"Amy, darling, go see if you can turn the cover down on your and little sister's crib, and help her in and tuck the cover around her good. It is so cold tonight, if I expose myself, Mamma will die.

Then fix the covers on Mamma's bed and you can go now and get in bed. Our fire is all out," I said. I was nursing my little infant in my lap.

"Mamma, don't you want me to put little brother to bed?" she asked.

"No, darling, Mamma will carry him. You might let him fall and kill him," I said. So, my two little angels went to bed and not a trouble of my heart disturbed their peaceful, innocent rest. I waited still and wondered, "Will I ever be happy?" My whole soul would then hover over my two little daughters. "Yes, they will someday be my comfort if we live, and here is my baby boy. Who knows but that he will bring me great honor and happiness in my declining days if God sees fit to spare us all. I must go to bed. I am getting cold, but I can never go to sleep. Oh, I know his horse has fell with him and he is lying crippled, or maybe killed, and no one to go after him. How I wish Mose or Eli was here to go see after him, but they are both gone. Well, I will lay my baby down and get ready for bed. I will set these light rolls there on the hearth to rise to bake for breakfast, too. Now I will lie down and wait."

So, I went to bed with a sad, heavy heart. I lay and listened. Way in the night he came. Oh, I was relieved when he opened the door. I had left my lamp burning and, when he opened the door, I raised up in bed. "Oh, Dave, I've been so uneasy. How come you so late? There is no fire for you to warm," I said. He gave no answer. "What have you been doing, Dave, that kept you so late?"

"Don't you go to giving me hell. I've had enough hell today," he said. He stormed out.

Oh, my heart sank within me. "Are you drunk, Dave?" I asked. He never spoke, but picked up the bucket of water and walked to the bedroom door and opened it and set the bucket down. "Dave, don't go in there to sleep. You will freeze. There is no cover on that bed." He gave me no answer, but went to bed in the room. I lay there in deep sorrow. "I can't get up in this cold room to cover him. It will kill me." I called Amy. "Amy, darling, get up and get some cover and cover Papa. He will freeze. He has gone to bed in the room." She was a very dutiful child, never returned a word when I told her to do a thing. She got cover and covered him and went to bed again.

When he went into the room, he slammed the door shut

after him and said, in hard words, "I wish to God I would die before morning."

It was like a dagger to my heart. What a great trouble and tumult arose in my soul. I tossed upon my pillow in tears, with supplication to the Lord to remove this evil habit from him.

In several hours he began calling me so pitifully, "Oh, Diden. Oh, Diden."

"What do you want, Dave?"

"Will you get me something to eat? I am starving to death," he said.

"Yes, Dave." I know it is cold, but I will risk it. I will get him something, I thought. I got up and went out through the dining room and on into the kitchen and found a pot of stewed beef. I brought it in and said, "Come to the hearth, Dave. It is so cold in that door where you are sitting."

"Oh, give me something to eat first and I will," he said.

I gave him a bone of beef and he ate like a ravenous wolf. I stood over him, begging him to come to the warm hearth. When he cleaned all the meat from the bone, he pitched the bone into the water bucket. "Oh, Dave, you threw it in the water bucket."

"Oh, did I?" he asked, reaching his hand in the water bucket after the bone.

"Oh, don't do that, Dave."

"Give me some more meat," he said.

"Come to the hearth and I will. You will die from cold sitting here." I coaxed him to the hearth and gave him another bone of beef.

"Now bring the water bucket here," he said.

I did so. There was only one chair near the hearth. I set it by him. "Sit in this chair, Dave."

"No, you take it," he said.

"No, Dave, you sit down and eat your meat."

"No, I'll sit down here," and down he sat.

"Oh, Dave, you have sat down on the light rolls."

"Oh, did I? I didn't aim to," he said. Up he got then and took the chair and cleaned the meat off of the second bone and pitched it into the water bucket.

"Oh, Dave, you threw that in the water bucket."

"Oh, did I?" and reached his hand into the water bucket at the same time and threw it on the floor.

"Oh, this is awful," I thought, but I felt so much relieved. We went to bed and I went to sleep. In a few minutes my burden had rolled away.

The next morning I began to think over what he had done. I couldn't help laughing. He saw me.

"Now, Diden, don't ever tell what a fool I acted last night. Will you not tell it?" he asked.

"I won't promise you that, Dave." I told him how he had done and mimicked him.

"Oh, my, I'm not fit to come in the house. Don't tell it for mercy's sake," he said.

Oliver came to see if he got in that morning. I began to tell him how he had done, but Dave held his hand over my mouth to prevent me from telling. I didn't get to tell all then, but did after awhile. He sobered up and went along smooth and alright. He went to town and back as sober as any man.

The next spring he planted a crop but the drouth came and cut it short, but he continued to plant every year. I wouldn't let him rest until he did plant. He saw after his stock after he planted the ground. He never took any interest in a crop, but I delighted in a farm. I was not able to work much in it, but always had it worked. We kept improving and taking in more land until we had a nice farm and fine tanks and all our land fenced; living very comfortable with our three children.

All our trouble was my bad health, but I had so much will power to strive and keep everything going, one never would think me to be an invalid to see my work and not see my stature, which was very frail, weighing from eighty-five to ninety pounds. But I went most of the time. I didn't see how I could stop until I took very ill, which was often the case, but as soon as I could possibly get up, I was going again.

My children were average for intelligence and I took a great deal of pains to train them. The two little girls gave me very little trouble, but Mathie was a very peculiar child; seemed to be inclined to want his way in spite of all I could do; had a wonderful mind. He learned his alphabet of the large letters by standing by me while I would be reading the Bible and asking me what each capital letter was. I always answered his questions, but never thought of impressing the alphabet on his mind until he knew it. I taught my oldest little girl at home, as we lived in a thinly settled neighborhood. Our schoolhouse was quite a distance off, too far for her to walk, her being six years old, but could read well and a fine speller.

Time passed with growing prosperity for us. I never worried so much now, except for my two youngest brothers out on the plains. I was always uneasy for fear they might get killed. I hadn't seen Eli since I left to make my trip to Arkansas. He got dissatisfied while I was gone and Dave gave him a horse and he went to where Jeff was on the plains. Now all three were there on the same ranch. I watched over them in spirit. Never a night passed that I didn't take their situations deep down in my heart and, oh, the tears I have shed over those boys.

The third year on our farm, we planted about four acres of cotton and Dave was gone on cowhunts most all spring. I thinned the cotton and kept the weeds down with a hoe until it began to bunch. He came in and I never let him rest until he plowed it. We made three bales of cotton and sold it at a fair price. Now I thought cotton was the thing. It brought the money. That winter another girl was born to us, little Myrtle, on the 26th day of December 1887. She weighed one and one-half pounds at her birth; an invalid. She was marked with different freaks of nature, which troubled me much and, being very frail and weak, it was a hard trial for me.

In January I was impressed of more trouble. Jeff and Eli were in; Jeff being married now and living at Richland and Eli was down there too. So Mose was all the one out. He remained on the ranch. I was troubled so deep, but I could not think Mose would get in trouble. He was loved by all that knew him, and so frank and familiar with everyone. It was his disposition. I often told him he oughtn't to be so. Ah, I never think any harm. They are all to me alike. So, I thought of him continually, and in January, the 24th day, we received a telegram that Mose was fatally wounded by a friend of his, Frank Drace.

This news was all I could bear, for I was very weak to bear such a shock. The telegram came to Jeff and he came quickly to me with the news. I saw vengeance in his eyes. He was on his way to going to Mose. "Oh, Jeff, don't kill Drace when you get there. If Mose is dead, it will only put you in trouble and you have a wife and child. Besides, oh me, I never can bear it," I said.

"Well, Diden, I can't say what I will do. I never would have thought of Frank shooting Mose. They were the best of friends and I never had a better friend than Drace. I know it was caused by Mose being too familiar with Frank's wife. He is so frank with everyone and Frank had no confidence in his wife and Mose lived with them, or took his meals there, and he lived in the little house where Jim was killed," he said.

"Well, Jeff, don't kill Drace when you get there," I said. I reasoned and pled as he left me.

All he said was, "I won't kill him now," but I saw murder in his eyes as he left me to go to Mose. If I ever looked to the Lord in sincerity, it was then.

The next day after Jeff left, we received a letter from one of the cowboys stating Mose was dead, only living three days after he was shot. Drace shot him three times. The first shot took effect through his kidneys, breaking his back, which disabled him to walk. Drace shot him from behind the corner of the little house Mose lived in. He had walked to the door, unaware of any danger, and was brutally murdered by a jealous friend. Drace told his wife that morning, if Mose did not leave he would kill him, and told his wife he was going hunting and took his gun and left, so she thought. No sooner than he was gone, she ran to the little house and found Mose writing.

"Mose, you will have to leave here. Frank is jealous of you and me," she said.

"Well, if that is the case, I will leave," he said. She went back to her house and Mose got up from his writing and was fixing to leave when he heard Mrs. Drace screaming. Mose thought Drace was whipping her and said he thought he would go and talk to Frank and picked up his pistol up off the table. When he stepped to the door, Drace shot him and broke his back and he fell in the door. Drace shot him twice after he fell, from behind the corner of the house.

When Mose said, "Frank, don't shoot me anymore. You have killed me without a cause, Frank. I never would have thought you would have done me so," he threw down his gun and called his wife to come. They carried him to their house and laid him on their bed and Mrs. Drace went eight miles on horseback to the nearest ranch after help. Drace stayed with Mose and did all he could for him, and talked and cried with sorrow deep, but too late. In about two hours one of the cowboys happened along and Drace went out of the house and left Starks with Mose.

"Starks, please give me my pistol. When Frank comes in, I will kill him," he said.

"Mose, I can't do that."

"Oh, please give me my pistol," he begged.

"Mose, I can't do that." When the boys came, Mose sent for Old Man Campbell, the owner of the Matador Ranch and a good friend of his. When he came, Mose had them take his testimony.

"Now this is all I have to say: I was murdered by a supposed friend. I want you to stay with me until I die."

Mr. Campbell said, "I will, Mose." He stayed with him and heard his last words. When Jeff got there, he had been buried several days. Drace was in custody. Jeff went to see him, but they kept a guard around him to protect him. He was like a maniac.

"Oh, I'll have him before I leave here," was Jeff's thought. So, he had the time and place planned to kill him the next day.

"Jeff, you go home with me tonight. I know your intentions and, in the morning, I will let you have all the money you need and I have a good shotgun you may have, too," Mr. Campbell said. So, the old man persuaded him to go home with him. As they journeyed along, the old man talked of his stock and his business matters. He was a moral man. So, finally he said, "Jeff, what church did your mother hold to?"

"The Christian Church," Jeff answered.

"How old was Mose when she died?" he asked.

"He was very young, only thirteen months old," Jeff said.

"Well, that is all I want to know. Jeff, I am a changed man. Just to think of that poor boy and what he said has changed me. Oh, I witnessed the agonies. It was terrible how he suffered. I stood over him until he ceased to suffer and I thought he was dead. All of a sudden, he looked me in the face. 'Mr. Campbell,' he said, laughing, 'Mother has come after me. Don't you hear her talking?'

'No, Mose. I don't hear anything.'

'Why, can't you hear her? Oh, what a shield I have now,' Mose said, and his spirit departed without a struggle."

All this time I was at home in deep distress, but the ears of the Lord are open to hear the pleadings of the righteous, and He works in many mysterious ways. So, when the old man told his story to Jeff, he said, "I felt like I wanted to waft away on a feather in the air. I felt so light and free. My sorrows were all gone. I would not hurt a hair on Drace's head." So, instead of killing Drace next morning, he started home a converted man.

When he took the stage at Goldthwaite for San Saba, the driver was drunk and swearing. "Old, man," said Jeff, "you are very old to use profane language like that," and told him the dying words of our brother.

He came home that night. "Sallie," he said to his wife, "I have something to tell, but won't tell it until I tell Diden." I sent Dave after him and his wife the next day. When I saw them they were near the gate. I stood in awe to hear the horrid news. I met him in the door.

"Oh, Jeff, tell me all about it."

Smiling, he said, "Diden, don't grieve. I want to tell you some good news and I know you will not grieve then," and I stopped suddenly and listened to the wonderful story.

I never believed anyone ever got overjoyed enough to produce shouting, but I was so overjoyed I shouted and gave thanks for His blessing He had bestowed on us to redeem my brother from deep despair.

Hope, New Mexico, February 14, 1906:

> On this blessed
> Valentine's Day
> there is some thoughts from my heart to say
> although the penalty of my heart may pay
> for taking advantage of Valentine's Day.
>
> While I sit alone and view all nature so divine,
> there is nothing so precious to this heart of mine
> as those winning eyes and that form of thine,
> awaiting patiently to be called your valentine.
>
> If all the world should frown on you
> and all love from others prove untrue,
> this love of mine shall always be thine,
> my love, my dearest valentine.

While this lobe of flesh within me strive,
watching and waiting the ebbing tide,
I am anxiously awaiting and watching the rise
that will drift you forever by my side.

This restless, aching heart of mine
is ever awaiting to be enshrined
with that true and protecting love of thine
when I can call you mine, my dearest valentine.

While I behold the great universe
and a thought I could not choose thee to converse,
my heart becomes so sad and weary
and my life so lonely and dreary.

Now I am sure thou will not refuse
for my love is pure and true;
nor will thou dare to deny
that my love is from on high.

Then think not in thy perfect mind
my love I will give to another in time.
If thou shouldst reject this sincere love of mine,
there is no other I would cast it on.
I shall always remain your true valentine.

Consider thou my poem well
and dare not my love from your heart expel.
It would cause the vibration of my heart to quell
And to all joy and happiness I would say farewell.

I shall leave you now. Hope you will decide
from whence this valentine came,
and not for one moment consider it vain
that thy pure heart might cast a shadow of blame.

> Your Valentine.
> by Mrs. Sarah C. Hall